THE AUSTRALIAN Women's Weekly
pressure cooker

acp books

The pressure cookers of today – both stove-top and electric – are completely safe and easy to use; their pressure regulators are much more refined than those used on the cookers of yesteryear. Read the instruction manual carefully before you start. Like most appliances, they all have slightly different features.

Both types of cookers, stove- and bench-top, work in the same way; the main difference is in the control of the appliance. The stove-top cooker needs the cook to control the pressure by controlling the heat source at the appropriate time, whereas the bench-top cooker does this work for you – it controls and adjusts the pressure. There is not a huge difference in price between the two types; the decision is yours.

Both cookers are quite large and bulky to store, the bench-top cooker of a similar capacity to a stove-top cooker will certainly be the larger of the two types and, once an appliance is put away in a cupboard, sadly, it often gets forgotten. Pressure cookers are not just for winter-time cooking; they're so handy for cooking many different foods all-year round that it seems a shame for them to be relegated to a cupboard. Consider the storage or bench space when you're choosing which size, shape and type to buy.

DO
- read your instruction manual thoroughly before you use the pressure cooker
- read cooking times carefully and begin to time the food after the pressure is reached
- fill the cooker up to the marked line inside the cooker – no more
- release the lid carefully, in an open space, facing away from you to avoid the escaping steam
- use a trivet – usually provided – for steaming puddings etc
- time your pressure cooking carefully – follow the recipes
- wash and dry the cooker and removable gasket well after use
- use a simmer mat to keep the heat as low as possible after a cooker has reached pressure
- use tongs – not your fingers – to release the pressure from the cooker
- wash the bases of pressure cookers in the dishwasher, after checking the manual
- store the cooker with its lid on upside-down

DON'T
- leave the cooker on and unattended
- over-fill the cooker with food and/or liquid
- cook pasta or porridge, or any food that becomes foamy in a pressure cooker
- soak the bases of pressure cookers
- wash the lid of a pressure cooker in a dishwasher – it will damage the valve

STOVE-TOP PRESSURE COOKERS

Stove-top cookers made from aluminium or stainless steel are suitable for either gas or electric cook tops, but you will need to buy stainless steel if you have either a ceramic or an induction stove-top. Price is a good guide to quality. The size and shape you choose will depend on your family's needs; if you're a soup-maker, think large. Do your research well and look at the cookers carefully; lift them to see if you can manage the weight and like the feel of the handle/s. Position the lids a few times to make sure you're comfortable with handling them. Also, consider that the cooker can be used in place of a saucepan or boiler, without the lid clamped in position. The lid can sit on top of the cooker similar to a saucepan lid if you like, making the cooker more versatile. When it's time to release the pressure of the cooker, do this off the heat.

THE QUICK RELEASE METHOD

For the quick release method referred to in our recipes use tongs (steam can burn your fingers) to turn the pressure valve on top of the cooker to open the valve and release the steam. This will release the pressure quickly, before you remove the lid. If you need to check the food towards the end of the suggested cooking time or add more ingredients to the cooker, follow the quick release method.

BENCH-TOP PRESSURE COOKERS

These cookers, once set, just get on with the job of reaching the required pressure then stabilising, before the cook steps in to release the pressure and remove the lid.

We used both a 6-litre (24-cup) and an 8-litre (32-cup) pressure cooker for the recipes in this book.

chicken and rice soup

2 teaspoons olive oil
1 large brown onion (200g), chopped finely
⅓ cup (65g) white long-grain rice
1 large tomato (220g), chopped finely
1 tablespoon drained, finely chopped, pickled
  jalapeño chillies
1 cup coarsely chopped fresh coriander (cilantro)
1 large avocado (320g), chopped finely

CHICKEN STOCK
½ chicken (800g)
1 medium carrot (120g), halved
1 small brown onion (80g), halved
1 stalk celery (150g), halved
1 teaspoon black peppercorns
1.5 litres (6 cups) water

1 Make chicken stock. Discard skin and bones from chicken; shred meat coarsely.
2 Heat oil in 6-litre (24-cup) pressure cooker; cook onion, stirring, until soft. Add rice; stir to coat in onion mixture. Add stock; secure lid. Bring cooker to high pressure. Reduce heat to stabilise pressure; cook 5 minutes.
3 Release pressure using the quick release method (page 6); remove lid. Return chicken to cooker with tomato and chilli; simmer, uncovered, until hot. Stir in coriander; season to taste. Serve soup topped with avocado.

CHICKEN STOCK Combine ingredients in 6-litre (24-cup) pressure cooker; secure lid. Bring cooker to high pressure. Reduce heat to stabilise pressure; cook 15 minutes. Release pressure using the quick release method (page 6); remove lid. Strain stock into large heatproof bowl. Reserve chicken; discard vegetables and pepper.

prep + cook time 30 minutes
makes 2.75 litres (11 cups)
nutritional count per 1 cup 11.4g total fat
(2.9g saturated fat); 698kJ (167 cal);
6.9g carbohydrate; 8.7g protein; 1.5g fibre

If you have an electric pressure cooker you won't need to reduce the heat to stabilise pressure, your cooker will automatically stabilise itself. Always check with the manufacturer's instructions before using. If making chicken stock for another recipe where you only need the stock, use chicken necks, wings and backs instead of the half chicken. The stock will keep refrigerated for up to 1 week, or frozen for up to 2 months.

scotch broth

1 tablespoon olive oil
1kg (2 pounds) lamb neck chops
½ cup (100g) pearl barley
1 large brown onion (200g), chopped coarsely
2 stalks celery (300g), trimmed, chopped coarsely
1 large carrot (180g), sliced thickly
1.5 litres (6 cups) water
3 cups (240g) finely shredded savoy cabbage
¾ cup coarsely chopped fresh flat-leaf parsley

1 Heat oil in 6-litre (24-cup) pressure cooker; cook lamb, in batches, until browned. Remove from cooker.
2 Return lamb to cooker with barley, onion, celery, carrot and the water; secure lid. Bring cooker to high pressure. Reduce heat to stabilise pressure; cook 20 minutes.
3 Release pressure using the quick release method (page 6); remove lid. Remove lamb with slotted spoon. Add cabbage to cooker; secure lid. Bring cooker to high pressure. Reduce heat to stabilise pressure; cook 5 minutes.
4 Meanwhile, remove meat from lamb chops; discard bones, chop meat coarsely.
5 Release pressure using the quick release method (page 6); remove lid. Stir in lamb and parsley; season to taste.

prep + cook time 40 minutes
makes 3 litres (12 cups)
nutritional count per 1 cup 9.5g total fat (3.7g saturated fat); 727kJ (174 cal); 7.4g carbohydrate; 13.6g protein; 2.8g fibre

If you have an electric pressure cooker you won't need to reduce the heat to stabilise pressure, your cooker will automatically stabilise itself. Always check with the manufacturer's instructions before using. Recipe suitable to freeze.

shredded beef and silver beet soup

1 tablespoon olive oil
1 medium brown onion (150g), chopped finely
2 cloves garlic, crushed
2 tablespoons tomato paste
¼ cup (60ml) dry red wine
1 litre (4 cups) water
410g (13 ounces) canned crushed tomatoes
500g (1 pound) piece beef skirt steak
2 dried bay leaves
3 medium silver beet (swiss chard) leaves (240g),
  trimmed, shredded coarsely

1   Heat oil in 6-litre (24-cup) pressure cooker; cook onion and garlic, stirring, until onion softens. Add paste; cook, stirring, 2 minutes. Add wine; simmer, uncovered, until liquid reduces by half. Add the water, undrained tomatoes, beef and bay leaves; secure lid. Bring cooker to high pressure. Reduce heat to stabilise pressure; cook 25 minutes.
2   Release pressure using the quick release method (page 6); remove lid. Discard bay leaves. Remove beef; when cool enough to handle, cut beef in half. Shred beef using two forks.
3   Return beef to soup with silver beet; simmer, uncovered, until silver beet wilts. Season to taste.

prep + cook time 45 minutes
makes 2 litres (8 cups)
nutritional count per 1 cup 4g total fat
(1g saturated fat); 506kJ (121 cal);
3.6g carbohydrate; 15.4g protein; 2g fibre

If you have an electric pressure cooker you won't need to reduce the heat to stabilise pressure, your cooker will automatically stabilise itself. Always check with the manufacturer's instructions before using. Recipe suitable to freeze.

harira

1 cup (200g) dried chickpeas (garbanzo beans)
2.5 litres (10 cups) water
2 tablespoons olive oil
2 french-trimmed lamb shanks (500g)
1 large brown onion (200g), chopped finely
3 cloves garlic, crushed
1 teaspoon ground cinnamon
½ teaspoon each ground turmeric and ginger
410g (13 ounces) canned diced tomatoes
½ cup (100g) brown lentils, rinsed, drained
¼ cup (60ml) lemon juice
1 cup coarsely chopped fresh coriander (cilantro)

1 Place chickpeas in medium bowl, cover with cold water; stand overnight. Rinse under cold water; drain.
2 Combine chickpeas and 3 cups (750ml) of the water in 6-litre (24-cup) pressure cooker; secure lid. Bring cooker to high pressure. Reduce heat to stabilise pressure; cook 10 minutes. Release pressure using the quick release method (page 6); remove lid. Drain chickpeas.
3 Heat oil in cooker; cook lamb until browned. Remove from cooker.

4 Cook onion and garlic in cooker, stirring, until onion softens. Add spices; cook, stirring, until fragrant. Return lamb to cooker with undrained tomatoes and the remaining water; secure lid. Bring cooker to high pressure. Reduce heat to stabilise pressure; cook 25 minutes.
5 Release pressure using the quick release method (page 6); remove lid. Add lentils and chickpeas; secure lid. Bring cooker to high pressure. Reduce heat to stabilise pressure; cook 15 minutes. Release pressure using the quick release method (page 6); remove lid. Remove lamb with slotted spoon.
6 When lamb is cool enough to handle, shred meat coarsely, discard bones. Return lamb to cooker with juice; simmer, uncovered, until hot. Season to taste. Serve soup topped with coriander.

prep + cook time 1 hour 10 minutes (+ standing)
makes 3 litres (12 cups)
nutritional count per 1 cup 5.6g total fat
(1.2g saturated fat); 606kJ (145 cal);
11.3g carbohydrate; 10.4g protein; 4.3g fibre

If you have an electric pressure cooker you won't need to reduce the heat to stabilise pressure, your cooker will automatically stabilise itself. Always check with the manufacturer's instructions before using. If you forget to, or can't soak the chickpeas overnight, simply cook them for 35 minutes instead of 10 in 6 cups of water instead of 3. You need to cook the chickpeas separately as they don't become tender if cooked with acid (tomatoes) or salt. Harira is a traditional Moroccan soup often served at night during Ramadan to break the fasting day. This recipe is suitable to freeze.

white bean and chorizo soup

1½ cups (300g) dried white beans
1.5 litres (6 cups) water
¼ cup (60ml) olive oil
4 cloves garlic, crushed
⅓ cup coarsely chopped fresh flat-leaf parsley
1 cured chorizo sausage (170g), halved
   lengthways, sliced thinly

1   Place beans in medium bowl, cover with cold water; stand overnight. Rinse under cold water; drain.
2   Combine beans and the water in 6-litre (24-cup) pressure cooker; secure lid. Bring cooker to high pressure. Reduce heat to stabilise pressure; cook 20 minutes. Release pressure using the quick release method (page 6); remove lid. Drain beans; reserve 3 cups (750ml) cooking liquid. Blend beans and reserved cooking liquid in batches until smooth.
3   Heat 2 tablespoons of the oil in cooker; stir in garlic, half the parsley and pureed beans. Simmer, uncovered, 5 minutes. Season to taste.
4   Meanwhile, heat remaining oil in large frying pan; cook chorizo until browned and crisp.
5   Serve soup topped with remaining parsley and chorizo; drizzle with chorizo cooking oil.

prep + cook time 35 minutes (+ standing)
makes 1.75 litres (7 cups)
nutritional count per 1 cup 16.1g total fat (3.9g saturated fat); 1170kJ (280 cal); 15.7g carbohydrate; 14.3g protein; 8.5g fibre

serving suggestion Serve with toasted bread.

If you have an electric pressure cooker you won't need to reduce the heat to stabilise pressure, your cooker will automatically stabilise itself. Always check the manufacturer's instructions before using. You can use dried cannellini, haricot or lima beans for this recipe. This recipe is not suitable to freeze.

chickpea, rice and yogurt soup

1 cup (200g) dried chickpeas (garbanzo beans)
2 litres (8 cups) water
½ cup (125ml) olive oil
2 large brown onions (400g), sliced thinly
1 cup (200g) jasmine rice
500g (1 pound) greek-style yogurt
1½ cups loosely packed fresh mint leaves

1 Place chickpeas in medium bowl, cover with cold water; stand overnight. Rinse under cold water; drain.
2 Combine chickpeas and half the water in 6-litre (24-cup) pressure cooker; secure lid. Bring cooker to high pressure. Reduce heat to stabilise pressure; cook 10 minutes.
3 Meanwhile, heat 2 tablespoons of the oil in large frying pan; cook onion, stirring, about 5 minutes until browned lightly. Reserve half the onion; cook remaining onion, stirring, about 8 minutes or until onion is caramelised.

4 Release pressure using the quick release method (page 6); remove lid. Stir in rice, reserved onion and the remaining water; secure lid. Bring cooker to high pressure. Reduce heat to stabilise pressure; cook 5 minutes. Release pressure using the quick release method (page 6); remove lid. Stir in yogurt; simmer, uncovered, until hot. Season to taste.
5 Meanwhile, heat remaining oil in small saucepan; deep-fry mint, in batches, until bright green. Remove with slotted spoon; drain on absorbent paper.
6 Serve bowls of soup topped with caramelised onion and fried mint.

prep + cook time 40 minutes (+ standing)
makes 2.5 litres (10 cups)
nutritional count per 1 cup 14.5g total fat (2.9g saturated fat); 1170kJ (280 cal); 27.9g carbohydrate; 7.9g protein; 3.8g fibre

If you have an electric pressure cooker you won't need to reduce the heat to stabilise pressure, your cooker will automatically stabilise itself. Always check with the manufacturer's instructions before using. If you forget to, or can't soak the chickpeas overnight, simply cook them for 35 minutes instead of 10 in 6 cups of water instead of 3. Step back from the stove when frying mint as it will spit. You can keep cooled fried leaves in an airtight container for up to 2 days. Recipe not suitable to freeze.

classic minestrone

1 ham hock (1kg)
1 medium brown onion (150g)
1 stalk celery (150g), trimmed, halved
1 teaspoon black peppercorns
1 dried bay leaf
1.5 litres (6 cups) water
2 cups (360g) cooked white beans
1 large carrot (180g), chopped coarsely
2 medium zucchini (240g), chopped coarsely
2 stalks celery (300g), chopped coarsely
3 cloves garlic, crushed
410g (13 ounces) canned diced tomatoes
1 cup (100g) small pasta shells
1 cup coarsely chopped fresh basil leaves
½ cup (40g) flaked parmesan cheese

1 Combine ham, onion, halved celery, peppercorns, bay leaf and the water in 6-litre (24-cup) pressure cooker; secure lid. Bring cooker to high pressure. Reduce heat to stabilise pressure; cook 20 minutes.

2 Release pressure using the quick release method (page 6); remove lid. Strain stock into large heatproof bowl; reserve ham, discard vegetables and peppercorns. When ham is cool enough to handle, remove meat from bone; discard bone, skin and fat, shred ham coarsely.

3 Return stock to cooker with shredded ham, beans, carrot, zucchini, chopped celery, garlic, undrained tomatoes and pasta; secure lid. Bring cooker to high pressure. Reduce heat to stabilise pressure; cook 3 minutes.

4 Release pressure using the quick release method (page 6); remove lid. Season to taste. Serve soup sprinkled with basil and cheese.

prep + cook time 35 minutes
makes 3.5 litres (14 cups)
nutritional count per 1 cup 3.4g total fat (1.4g saturated fat); 581kJ (139 cal); 11.4g carbohydrate; 14.2g protein; 3.6g fibre

If you have an electric pressure cooker you won't need to reduce the heat to stabilise pressure, your cooker will automatically stabilise itself. Always check with the manufacturer's instructions before using. You'll need to cook 1 cup (200g) of dried white beans for this recipe. If soaked overnight, they take 10 minutes to cook in a pressure cooker. You can use any white bean you like. Recipe not suitable to freeze.

lamb shank, vegetable and lentil soup

2 tablespoons olive oil
3 french-trimmed lamb shanks (750g)
1 medium brown onion (150g), chopped finely
2 cloves garlic, crushed
2 medium carrots (240g), chopped coarsely
2 celery stalks (300g), trimmed, chopped coarsely
155g (5 ounces) piece of pancetta,
  chopped coarsely
1.25 litres (5 cups) water
½ cup (125ml) dry white wine
⅔ cup (130g) french-style green lentils,
  rinsed, drained
½ cup (60g) frozen peas

1 Heat half the oil in 6-litre (24-cup) pressure cooker; cook lamb, in batches, until browned. Remove from cooker.
2 Heat remaining oil in cooker; cook onion, garlic, carrot, celery and pancetta, stirring, until vegetables soften. Return lamb to cooker with the water and wine; secure lid. Bring cooker to high pressure. Reduce heat to stabilise pressure; cook 20 minutes.
3 Release pressure using the quick release method (page 6); remove lid. Add lentils; secure lid. Bring cooker to high pressure. Reduce heat to stabilise pressure; cook 10 minutes.
4 Release pressure using the quick release method (page 6); remove lid. Remove lamb; when cool enough to handle shred meat coarsely, discard bones. Return lamb to cooker with peas; simmer, uncovered until peas are tender. Season to taste.

prep + cook time 40 minutes
makes 2 litres (8 cups)
nutritional count per 1 cup 10.5g total fat (3g saturated fat); 957kJ (229 cal); 9.5g carbohydrate; 19.6g protein; 4.2g fibre

If you have an electric pressure cooker you won't need to reduce the heat to stabilise pressure, your cooker will automatically stabilise itself. Always check with the manufacturer's instructions before using. Recipe suitable to freeze.

pea, ham and broad bean soup

1 tablespoon olive oil
1 large brown onion (200g), chopped coarsely
2 cloves garlic, crushed
2 celery stalks (300g), trimmed, chopped coarsely
1 medium carrot (120g), chopped coarsely
1 ham hock (750g)
2 dried bay leaves
2 litres (8 cups) water
1½ cups (225g) frozen broad beans
  (fava beans), peeled
1½ cups (300g) green split peas, rinsed, drained

MINT SAUCE
2 cups loosely packed fresh mint leaves
¼ cup (60ml) olive oil
2 tablespoons white wine vinegar
2 teaspoons caster (superfine) sugar

1 Heat oil in 6-litre (24-cup) pressure cooker; cook onion, garlic, celery and carrot, stirring, about 3 minutes or until vegetables soften. Add ham, bay leaves and the water; secure lid. Bring cooker to high pressure. Reduce heat to stabilise pressure; cook 20 minutes.
2 Release pressure using the quick release method (page 6); remove lid. Add beans and peas; secure lid. Bring cooker to high pressure. Reduce heat to stabilise pressure; cook 20 minutes.
3 Release pressure using the quick release method (page 6); remove lid. Discard bay leaves. Remove ham. Cool soup 10 minutes.
4 Meanwhile, discard skin, fat and bone from ham; shred meat coarsely.
5 Blend or process soup, in batches, until smooth. Return soup to cooker; stir in ham. Simmer, uncovered, until hot; season to taste.
6 Meanwhile, make mint sauce.
7 Serve bowls of soup drizzled with mint sauce.

MINT SAUCE Blend ingredients until smooth.

prep + cook time 1 hour 10 minutes
makes 1.5 litres (6 cups)
nutritional count per 1 cup 18.3g total fat
(3.5g saturated fat); 1751kJ (419 cal);
32g carbohydrate; 26.1g protein; 11.1g fibre

If you have an electric pressure cooker you won't need to reduce the heat to stabilise pressure, your cooker will automatically stabilise itself. Always check with the manufacturer's instructions before using. Soup suitable to freeze; mint sauce not suitable to freeze.

chicken

coq au vin

12 baby brown onions (300g)
2 tablespoons olive oil
3 rindless bacon slices (195g), chopped coarsely
315g (10 ounces) button mushrooms
3 cloves garlic, crushed
2 tablespoons plain (all-purpose) flour
4 chicken thigh cutlets (800g)
4 chicken drumsticks (600g)
¼ cup (70g) tomato paste
1 cup (250ml) dry red wine
2 dried bay leaves
6 sprigs fresh thyme

1 Peel onions, leaving root ends intact. Heat
2 teaspoons of the oil in 6-litre (24-cup) pressure
cooker; cook onions, stirring, until browned lightly.
Remove from cooker.
2 Heat another 2 teaspoons of the oil in cooker;
cook bacon, mushrooms and garlic, stirring, until
browned lightly. Remove from cooker.

3 Season flour in large bowl; add chicken, toss to
coat in flour. Shake off excess. Heat remaining oil in
cooker; cook chicken, in batches, until browned.
Remove from cooker.
4 Return chicken to cooker with onions, bacon
mixture, paste, wine, bay leaves and thyme; secure
lid. Bring cooker to high pressure. Reduce heat to
stabilise pressure; cook 10 minutes.
5 Release pressure using the quick release
method (page 6); remove lid. Season to taste;
serve sprinkled with thyme leaves.

prep + cook time 30 minutes **serves** 4
nutritional count per serving 47.7g total fat
(13.9g saturated fat); 3035kJ (726 cal);
10g carbohydrate; 53.5g protein; 2.2g fibre

serving suggestion Serve with mashed potato.

If you have an electric pressure cooker you won't
need to reduce the heat to stabilise pressure,
your cooker will automatically stabilise itself.
Always check with the manufacturer's instructions
before using. Recipe not suitable to freeze.

green chicken curry

1 tablespoon peanut oil
1kg (2 pounds) chicken thigh fillets, quartered
¼ cup (75g) green curry paste
1 cup (250ml) coconut cream
2 medium zucchini (240g), sliced thickly
1 tablespoon fish sauce
1 tablespoon lime juice
1 tablespoon grated palm sugar
⅓ cup each loosely packed fresh coriander
  (cilantro) and thai basil leaves
2 green onions (scallions), sliced thinly

1 Heat half the oil in 6-litre (24-cup) pressure
cooker; cook chicken, in batches, until browned.
Remove from cooker.
2 Heat remaining oil in cooker; cook paste,
stirring, about 3 minutes or until fragrant. Return
chicken to cooker with coconut cream; secure lid.
Bring cooker to high pressure. Reduce heat to
stabilise pressure; cook 5 minutes.
3 Release pressure using the quick release
method (page 6); remove lid. Add zucchini; secure
lid. Bring cooker to high pressure. Reduce heat to
stabilise pressure; cook 2 minutes.
4 Release pressure using the quick release
method (page 6); remove lid. Stir in sauce, juice,
sugar and half the herbs; season to taste. Serve
sprinkled with remaining herbs and onion.

prep + cook time 20 minutes **serves** 4
nutritional count per serving 41.6g total fat
(18.3g saturated fat); 2562kJ (613 cal);
8.6g carbohydrate; 50.1g protein; 4.4g fibre

serving suggestion Serve with steamed jasmine rice.

If you have an electric pressure cooker you won't
need to reduce the heat to stabilise pressure,
your cooker will automatically stabilise itself.
Always check with the manufacturer's instructions
before using. Recipe not suitable to freeze.

chicken and fig tagine

2 tablespoons plain (all-purpose) flour
4 single chicken breasts on the bone (1kg)
2 tablespoons olive oil
1 large red onion (300g), sliced thinly
2 cloves garlic, crushed
2 teaspoons each ground cumin, coriander, ginger
  and cinnamon
pinch saffron threads
¾ cup (180ml) chicken stock
1 tablespoon honey
315g (10 ounces) spinach, trimmed,
  shredded coarsely
6 medium fresh figs (360g), halved
1 teaspoon caster (superfine) sugar
2 tablespoons each coarsely chopped fresh
  flat-leaf parsley and coriander (cilantro)
½ cup (70g) coarsely chopped, roasted
  unsalted pistachios

1 Season flour in large bowl; add chicken, toss to coat in flour. Shake off excess. Heat half the oil in 6-litre (24-cup) pressure cooker; cook chicken, in batches, until browned. Remove from cooker.
2 Heat remaining oil in cooker; cook onion, garlic and spices, stirring, until onion softens. Return chicken to cooker with stock and honey; secure lid. Bring cooker to high pressure. Reduce heat to stabilise pressure; cook 15 minutes.
3 Release pressure using the quick release method (page 6); remove lid. Remove chicken; cover to keep warm. Stir spinach into cooker; season to taste.
4 Place figs, cut-side up, on baking paper-lined oven tray; sprinkle with sugar. Cook under preheated grill about 5 minutes or until browned lightly.
5 Return chicken to cooker; simmer, uncovered, until hot. Serve tagine topped with figs; sprinkle with herbs and nuts.

prep + cook time 30 minutes **serves** 4
nutritional count per serving 39g total fat
(8.5g saturated fat); 2742kJ (656 cal);
25.9g carbohydrate; 48g protein; 7.5g fibre

If you have an electric pressure cooker you won't need to reduce the heat to stabilise pressure, your cooker will automatically stabilise itself. Always check with the manufacturer's instructions before using. Recipe suitable to freeze without figs.

chicken, pear and sage stew

1 tablespoon olive oil
4 chicken thigh cutlets (800g)
40g (1½ ounces) butter
1 medium leek (350g), sliced thinly
2 cloves garlic, crushed
⅓ cup (80ml) verjuice
¾ cup (180ml) chicken stock
8 fresh sage leaves
2 medium parsnips (500g), quartered
2 medium firm pears (460g), peeled,
  cored, quartered
¼ cup loosely packed fresh sage leaves, extra

1 Heat oil in 6-litre (24-cup) pressure cooker; cook chicken, in batches, until browned. Remove chicken from cooker.
2 Melt half the butter in cooker; cook leek and garlic, stirring, until leek softens. Return chicken to cooker with verjuice, stock and sage; secure lid. Bring cooker to high pressure. Reduce heat to stabilise pressure; cook 10 minutes.
3 Release pressure using the quick release method (page 6); remove lid. Add parsnip and pear; secure lid. Bring cooker to high pressure. Reduce heat to stabilise pressure; cook 5 minutes.
4 Meanwhile, melt remaining butter in small frying pan; cook extra sage leaves until bright green and crisp. Drain on absorbent paper.
5 Release pressure using the quick release method (page 6); remove lid. Season to taste. Serve stew sprinkled with crisp sage leaves.

prep + cook time 30 minutes **serves** 4
nutritional count per serving 33.5g total fat
(12.7g saturated fat); 2199kJ (526 cal);
26.2g carbohydrate; 27.4g protein; 6.3g fibre

If you have an electric pressure cooker you won't need to reduce the heat to stabilise pressure, your cooker will automatically stabilise itself. Always check with the manufacturer's instructions before using. Make sure you use firm pears for this recipe or they will become mushy. Store crisp sage leaves in an airtight container for up to two days. Stew suitable to freeze.

chicken with capsicum

1 tablespoon olive oil
4 chicken thigh cutlets (800g)
2 medium brown onions (300g), sliced thinly
3 cloves garlic, crushed
2 medium red capsicums (bell peppers)
  (400g), sliced thickly
2 medium yellow capsicums (bell peppers)
  (400g), sliced thickly
1 tablespoon tomato paste
⅓ cup (80ml) dry white wine
⅓ cup (80ml) chicken stock
2 dried bay leaves
4 sprigs fresh thyme
2 teaspoons finely chopped fresh thyme

1 Heat half the oil in 6-litre (24-cup) pressure cooker; cook chicken, in batches, until browned. Remove from cooker.
2 Heat remaining oil in cooker; cook onion, garlic and capsicum, stirring, until onion softens. Add paste; cook, stirring, 1 minute. Return chicken to cooker with wine, stock, bay leaves and thyme sprigs; secure lid. Bring cooker to high pressure. Reduce heat to stabilise pressure; cook 15 minutes.
3 Release pressure using the quick release method (page 6); remove lid. Season to taste. Serve sprinkled with chopped thyme.

prep + cook time 30 minutes serves 4
nutritional count per serving 25g total fat
(7.3g saturated fat); 1634kJ (391 cal);
10.1g carbohydrate; 27g protein; 3g fibre

serving suggestion Serve with mashed potatoes.

If you have an electric pressure cooker you won't need to reduce the heat to stabilise pressure, your cooker will automatically stabilise itself. Always check with the manufacturer's instructions before using. Recipe suitable to freeze.

greek-style roast chicken

1.6kg (3¼-pound) whole chicken
1 medium lemon (140g), cut into wedges
6 cloves garlic, unpeeled
6 sprigs fresh oregano
1 tablespoon olive oil
1 cup (250ml) chicken stock
½ cup (125ml) dry white wine

1 Rinse chicken under cold water; pat dry. Push lemon, garlic and oregano into chicken cavity. Tuck wing tips under; tie legs together with kitchen string. Season.
2 Heat oil in 6-litre (24-cup) pressure cooker; cook chicken until browned all over. Remove from cooker. Add stock and wine to cooker; place chicken on oiled wire rack in cooker. Secure lid; bring cooker to high pressure. Reduce heat to stabilise pressure; cook 30 minutes.
3 Release pressure using the quick release method (page 6); remove lid. Remove chicken, cover; stand 10 minutes before serving. Discard cooking liquid or reserve for use as stock.

prep + cook time 45 minutes serves 6
nutritional count per serving 24.8g total fat (7.2g saturated fat); 1463kJ (350 cal); 1.1g carbohydrate; 27.4g protein; 1.1g fibre

If you have an electric pressure cooker you won't need to reduce the heat to stabilise pressure, your cooker will automatically stabilise itself. Always check with the manufacturer's instructions before using. Recipe not suitable to freeze.

steak and kidney pie

¼ cup (60ml) olive oil
200g (6½ ounces) swiss brown
  mushrooms, quartered
400g (12½ ounces) ox kidney, trimmed,
  chopped coarsely
2 tablespoons plain (all-purpose) flour
700g (1½ pounds) beef chuck steak,
  chopped coarsely
1 medium brown onion (150g), chopped finely
1 large carrot (180g), chopped finely
1 stalk celery (150g), trimmed, chopped finely
2 sprigs fresh thyme
1 dried bay leaf
⅓ cup (80ml) water
1 sheet ready-rolled puff pastry
1 egg, beaten lightly

1 Heat 2 teaspoons of the oil in 6-litre (24-cup) pressure cooker; cook mushrooms until browned. Remove from cooker.
2 Heat 2 teaspoons of the oil in cooker; cook kidney until browned. Remove from cooker.
3 Season flour in large bowl; add beef, toss to coat in flour. Shake off excess. Heat half the remaining oil in cooker; cook beef, in batches, until browned. Remove from cooker.
4 Heat remaining oil in cooker; cook onion, carrot and celery, stirring, until tender. Return beef to cooker with thyme, bay leaf and the water; secure lid. Bring cooker to high pressure. Reduce heat to stabilise pressure; cook 25 minutes.
5 Meanwhile, preheat oven to 210°C/415°F.
6 Release pressure using the quick release method (page 6); remove lid, discard thyme and bay leaf. Stir in mushrooms and drained kidney; season to taste. Spoon hot steak and kidney mixture into 1.5-litre (6-cup) deep ovenproof pie dish. Place pastry over filling, trim edge; cut two small slits in centre of pastry. Brush pastry with egg. Bake pie about 25 minutes or until well browned.

prep + cook time 1 hour 10 minutes **serves** 4
nutritional count per serving 35g total fat
(7.2g saturated fat); 2755kJ (659 cal);
24.3g carbohydrate; 60g protein; 4.1g fibre

If you have an electric pressure cooker you won't need to reduce the heat to stabilise pressure, your cooker will automatically stabilise itself. Always check with the manufacturer's instructions before using. Steak and kidney filling is suitable to freeze.

chilli con carne

2 cups (400g) dried red kidney beans
3 small brown onions (240g)
1 dried bay leaf
1.5 litres (6 cups) water
150g (4½ ounces) speck, chopped finely
1 cured chorizo sausage (170g), chopped finely
400g (12½ ounces) minced (ground) beef
2 cloves garlic, crushed
2 tablespoons ground cumin
1 tablespoon ground coriander
1 teaspoon dried chilli flakes
2 cups (560g) bottled tomato pasta sauce
2 teaspoons dried oregano
½ cup (120g) sour cream
½ cup loosely packed fresh coriander
  (cilantro) leaves

1   Place beans in large bowl, cover with cold water; stand overnight. Rinse under cold water; drain.
2   Combine beans, one of the onions, bay leaf and the water in 6-litre (24-cup) pressure cooker; secure lid. Bring cooker to high pressure. Reduce heat to stabilise pressure; cook 15 minutes. Release pressure using the quick release method (page 6); remove lid. Drain beans, reserving 1½ cups (375ml) cooking liquid; discard onion and bay leaf.
3   Finely chop remaining onions. Cook speck and chorizo in cooker until browned. Add onion; cook, stirring, until onion softens. Add beef; cook, stirring, until browned. Add garlic and spices; cook, stirring, until fragrant. Return beans to cooker with sauce, oregano and reserved cooking liquid; season to taste. Bring cooker to high pressure. Reduce heat to stabilise pressure; cook 8 minutes. Release pressure using the quick release method (page 6); remove lid. Stand 5 minutes.
4   Serve chilli con carne with sour cream and sprinkled with coriander.

prep + cook time 40 minutes (+ standing) **serves** 6
nutritional count per serving 34.9g total fat (15.3g saturated fat); 2913kJ (697 cal); 36.1g carbohydrate; 51.3g protein; 17.1g fibre

If you have an electric pressure cooker you won't need to reduce the heat to stabilise pressure, your cooker will automatically stabilise itself. Always check with the manufacturer's instructions before using. If you normally eat chilli con carne with sour cream but are trying to be good, try it with a dollop of light greek-style yogurt. Recipe suitable to freeze.

beef cheeks with red wine

12 baby brown onions (300g)
2 tablespoons olive oil
2 tablespoons plain (all-purpose) flour
1kg (2 pounds) beef cheeks, chopped coarsely
1 dried bay leaf
3 sprigs fresh parsley
1 sprig fresh thyme
1 large brown onion (200g), chopped finely
3 cloves garlic, crushed
½ cup (125ml) dry red wine
¼ cup (60ml) water
3 large carrots (540g), chopped coarsely
1½ tablespoons balsamic vinegar glaze

1   Peel baby onions, leaving root ends intact. Heat 2 teaspoons of the oil in 6-litre (24-cup) pressure cooker; cook baby onions, stirring, about 5 minutes or until browned lightly all over. Remove from cooker.

2   Season flour in large bowl; add beef, toss to coat in flour. Shake off excess. Heat 1 tablespoon of the oil in cooker; cook beef, in batches, until browned. Remove from cooker.

3   Tie bay leaf, parsley and thyme together with kitchen string to make a bouquet garni. Heat remaining oil in cooker; cook chopped onion and garlic, stirring, until onion softens. Return beef to cooker with wine, the water and bouquet garni; secure lid. Bring cooker to high pressure. Reduce heat to stabilise pressure; cook 20 minutes.

4   Release pressure using the quick release method (page 6); remove lid. Add baby onions and carrots; secure lid. Bring cooker to high pressure. Reduce heat to stabilise pressure; cook 5 minutes. Release pressure using the quick release method (page 6); remove lid. Stir in glaze; season to taste. Serve sprinkled with chopped parsley if you like.

prep + cook time 50 minutes serves 6
nutritional count per serving 19.5g total fat (6.5g saturated fat); 1626kJ (389 cal); 11.3g carbohydrate; 36.9g protein; 3.7g fibre

serving suggestion Serve with mashed potatoes and your favourite steamed green vegetables.

If you have an electric pressure cooker you won't need to reduce the heat to stabilise pressure, your cooker will automatically stabilise itself. Always check with the manufacturer's instructions before using. You can use chuck or gravy beef for this recipe, but beef cheek is an amazing cut of meat; cooked long enough (or in a pressure cooker) it melts in your mouth. Recipe suitable to freeze.

beef tagine with spinach and olives

1 tablespoon olive oil
1.2kg (2½ pounds) beef blade steak, trimmed,
   chopped coarsely
1 medium brown onion (150g), chopped finely
2 cloves garlic, crushed
1 teaspoon each ground allspice and dried
   chilli flakes
pinch saffron threads
410g (13 ounces) canned crushed tomatoes
½ cup (125ml) beef stock
300g (9½ ounces) spinach, trimmed,
   shredded coarsely
½ cup (60g) seeded green olives
2 tablespoons thinly sliced preserved lemon rind
⅓ cup (45g) coarsely chopped, roasted
   unsalted pistachios

1 Heat half the oil in 6-litre (24-cup) pressure
cooker; cook beef, in batches, until browned.
Remove from cooker.
2 Heat remaining oil in cooker; cook onion, garlic
and spices, stirring, until onion softens. Return beef
to cooker with undrained tomatoes and stock;
secure lid. Bring cooker to high pressure. Reduce
heat to stabilise pressure; cook 15 minutes.
3 Release pressure using the quick release
method (page 6); remove lid. Stir in spinach, olives
and preserved lemon; simmer, uncovered, until hot.
Season to taste.
4 Serve tagine sprinkled with nuts.

prep + cook time 30 minutes **serves** 4
nutritional count per serving 30.5g total fat
(9.8g saturated fat); 2537kJ (607 cal);
11.3g carbohydrate; 69g protein; 5.4g fibre

serving suggestion Serve with couscous.

If you have an electric pressure cooker you won't
need to reduce the heat to stabilise pressure,
your cooker will automatically stabilise itself.
Always check with the manufacturer's instructions
before using. Recipe not suitable to freeze.

corned beef

1.5kg (3-pound) piece corned beef silverside
1 medium brown onion (150g),
  chopped coarsely
2 dried bay leaves
6 black peppercorns
1 medium carrot (120g), chopped coarsely
1 celery stalk (150g), trimmed, chopped coarsely
2 tablespoons light brown sugar
2 tablespoons malt vinegar
1.5 litres (6 cups) water, approximately

1 Combine beef, onion, bay leaves, peppercorns, carrot, celery, sugar, vinegar and enough of the water to barely cover beef in 6-litre (24-cup) pressure cooker; secure lid. Bring cooker to high pressure. Reduce heat to stabilise pressure; cook 45 minutes.
2 Release pressure using the quick release method (page 6); remove lid. Stand beef in cooking liquid 15 minutes. Remove beef from cooker. Serve sliced, warm or cold.

prep + cook time 1 hour (+ standing) **serves** 6
nutritional count per serving 7.1g total fat (3g saturated fat); 1116kJ (267 cal); 6.7g carbohydrate; 43.1g protein; 1.1g fibre

serving suggestion Serve warm corned beef with creamy mashed potato, mustard, cornichons, caperberries and parsley or with steamed potatoes, carrots and cabbage. Serve thin slices of cold corned beef on sandwiches with pickles.

If you have an electric pressure cooker you won't need to reduce the heat to stabilise pressure, your cooker will automatically stabilise itself. Always check with the manufacturer's instructions before using. If corned beef is to be served cold, cool the beef in the cooking liquid before refrigerating. Recipe not suitable to freeze.

chinese braised oxtail

1kg (2 pounds) beef oxtail, trimmed
½ cup (125ml) japanese soy sauce
¼ cup (60ml) chinese cooking wine
¼ cup (55g) firmly packed dark brown sugar
6 cloves garlic, bruised
12cm (4¾-inch) piece fresh ginger (60g), peeled,
  sliced thickly
4 green onions (scallions), chopped coarsely
2 star anise
2 cinnamon sticks
3 x 5cm (2-inch) strips orange rind
½ cup (125ml) water
2 green onions (scallions), shredded finely

1 Cut oxtail into 4cm (1½-inch) pieces. Combine sauce, wine, sugar, garlic, ginger, chopped onion, star anise, cinnamon, rind and the water in 6-litre (24-cup) pressure cooker; bring to the boil. Add oxtail; secure lid. Bring cooker to high pressure. Reduce heat to stabilise pressure; cook 30 minutes.
2 Release pressure using the quick release method (page 6); remove lid. Transfer oxtail to serving plate; drizzle with about ⅓ cup (80ml) of braising liquid. Sprinkle with shredded onion.

prep + cook time 40 minutes **serves** 4
nutritional count per serving 67.2g total fat (25.8g saturated fat); 3595kJ (860 cal); 16.8g carbohydrate; 46g protein; 1.6g fibre

serving suggestion Serve with steamed rice and asian greens.

If you have an electric pressure cooker you won't need to reduce the heat to stabilise pressure, your cooker will automatically stabilise itself. Always check with the manufacturer's instructions before using. We prefer the light flavour of the japanese soy sauce in this recipe. This recipe is suitable to freeze.

beef rendang

2 tablespoons vegetable oil
1kg (2 pounds) gravy beef, chopped coarsely
4cm (1½-inch) piece fresh galangal (20g), grated
⅔ cup (160ml) coconut milk
2 x 10cm (4-inch) sticks fresh lemon grass
   (40g), bruised
½ cup (125ml) water
½ cup (40g) toasted shredded coconut

SPICE PASTE
6 shallots (150g), chopped coarsely
4 fresh long red chillies, chopped coarsely
6cm (2¼-inch) piece fresh ginger (30g), grated
4cm (1½-inch) piece fresh turmeric (20g)
   sliced thinly
4 cloves garlic, quartered
3 teaspoons ground coriander

1 Make spice paste.
2 Heat oil in 6-litre (24-cup) pressure cooker; cook beef, in batches, until browned. Remove from cooker.
3 Return beef to cooker with spice paste and galangal; cook, stirring, about 2 minutes or until fragrant. Add coconut milk, lemon grass and the water; secure lid. Bring cooker to high pressure. Reduce heat to stabilise pressure; cook 45 minutes.
4 Release pressure using the quick release method (page 6); remove lid. Discard lemon grass; season to taste. Serve curry sprinkled with coconut.

SPICE PASTE Blend or process ingredients until mixture forms a thick paste.

prep + cook time 1 hour 10 minutes serves 6
nutritional count per serving 29.2g total fat (15.5g saturated fat); 1760kJ (421 cal); 2.8g carbohydrate; 36.1g protein; 2.3g fibre

serving suggestion Serve with steamed basmati rice.

If you have an electric pressure cooker you won't need to reduce the heat to stabilise pressure, your cooker will automatically stabilise itself. Always check with the manufacturer's instructions before using. If fresh turmeric is unavailable, replace it with ½ teaspoon ground turmeric. Bruise the white part of the lemon grass by squashing it gently with the flat part of a large knife. If you prefer the curry more moist, drizzle with a little warmed coconut milk at serving time. Recipe suitable to freeze.

italian-braised beef with white beans

1 cup (200g) dried white beans
2 tablespoons olive oil
4-cutlet beef rib roast (1.7kg)
2 tablespoons wholegrain mustard
4 cloves garlic, crushed
2 teaspoons smoked paprika
¼ cup finely chopped fresh flat-leaf parsley
1 medium brown onion (150g),
  chopped coarsely
½ teaspoon dried chilli flakes
¼ cup finely chopped fresh basil
410g (13 ounces) canned crushed tomatoes
1½ cups (375ml) beef stock

1   Place beans in medium bowl, cover with cold water; stand overnight. Rinse under cold water; drain.
2   Heat 2 teaspoons of the oil in 6-litre (24-cup) pressure cooker; cook beef until browned all over. Remove from cooker.
3   Combine 1 tablespoon of the oil, mustard, half the garlic, paprika and parsley in small bowl; rub mustard mixture all over beef.

4   Heat remaining oil in cooker; cook onion, remaining garlic, chilli and half the basil, stirring, until onion softens. Add beans, undrained tomatoes and stock; top with beef. Secure lid; bring cooker to high pressure. Reduce heat to stabilise pressure; cook 30 minutes.
5   Release pressure using the quick release method (page 6); remove lid. Remove beef, cover; stand 10 minutes. Stir remaining basil into bean mixture. Serve beef with beans.

prep + cook time 50 minutes **serves** 4
nutritional count per serving 32.5g total fat (11g saturated fat); 3143kJ (752 cal); 25.9g carbohydrate; 85.1g protein; 12g fibre

serving suggestion Serve with a green salad or steamed green vegetables.

If you have an electric pressure cooker you won't need to reduce the heat to stabilise pressure, your cooker will automatically stabilise itself. Always check with the manufacturer's instructions before using. We used cannellini beans in this recipe but you can use any dried white beans you like. This is a large serving of meat. Cooking time is for medium to well-done beef. Cook more or less depending on how you like your beef. You will find the mustard in this recipe means you won't need to season the meal. Recipe not suitable to freeze.

lamb

herb and mustard lamb leg

2 tablespoons olive oil
½ small brown onion (40g), chopped finely
2 cloves garlic, crushed
1 rindless bacon slice (65g), chopped finely
50g (1½ ounces) button mushrooms,
  chopped finely
2 tablespoons finely chopped fresh flat-leaf parsley
2 teaspoons finely chopped fresh rosemary
1 tablespoon wholegrain mustard
⅓ cup (35g) packaged breadcrumbs
1 egg, beaten lightly
1.4kg (2¾-pound) easy-carve lamb leg
½ cup (125ml) chicken stock
½ cup (125ml) dry white wine

1 Heat half the oil in large frying pan; cook onion, garlic, bacon and mushrooms, stirring, until onion softens and bacon is crisp. Remove from pan; cool.
2 Combine onion mixture, herbs, mustard, breadcrumbs and egg in medium bowl; season.
3 Open lamb leg out on board; slice through thickest part of lamb horizontally, without cutting all the way through, to make flap. Press breadcrumb mixture down centre of lamb cavity. Roll lamb tightly to enclose filling; tie lamb, at 2cm (¾-inch) intervals, with kitchen string to secure.

4 Heat remaining oil in pan; cook lamb until browned all over. Transfer lamb to 8-litre (32-cup) pressure cooker. Add stock and wine to cooker; secure lid. Bring cooker to high pressure. Reduce heat to stabilise pressure; cook 25 minutes.
5 Release pressure using the quick release method (page 6); remove lid. Remove lamb, cover; stand 10 minutes before slicing. Serve the lamb with pan juices.

prep + cook time 45 minutes serves 6
nutritional count per serving 17.8g total fat (6.3g saturated fat); 1509kJ (361 cal); 4.8g carbohydrate; 41.7g protein; 0.19g fibre

serving suggestion Serve lamb with steamed buttered vegetables, mashed potato and gravy. Leftover sliced lamb would be delicious on crusty bread rolls with some rocket (arugula) and tomato chutney or mustard.

If you have an electric pressure cooker you won't need to reduce the heat to stabilise pressure, your cooker will automatically stabilise itself. Always check with the manufacturer's instructions before using. Recipe not suitable to freeze. The lamb will be medium after the 25 minutes. If you prefer it less pink, cook for 30 minutes.

lamb navarin

1 tablespoon olive oil
4 lamb neck chops (680g), trimmed
1 large brown onion (200g), chopped finely
2 cloves garlic, crushed
410g (13 ounces) canned diced tomatoes
½ cup (125ml) water
8 baby brown onions (200g)
500g (1 pound) baby new potatoes, halved
400g (12½ ounces) baby carrots, trimmed, peeled
1 cup (120g) frozen peas
2 tablespoons coarsely chopped fresh
   flat-leaf parsley

1 Heat oil in 6-litre (24-cup) pressure cooker; cook lamb, in batches, until browned. Remove from cooker.
2 Cook chopped onion and garlic in cooker, stirring, until onion softens. Return lamb to cooker with undrained tomatoes and the water; secure lid. Bring cooker to high pressure. Reduce heat to stabilise pressure; cook 15 minutes.
3 Meanwhile, peel baby onions, leaving root ends intact.
4 Release cooker pressure using the quick release method (page 6); remove lid. Stir in potato and onions, top with carrots; secure lid. Bring cooker to high pressure. Reduce heat to stabilise pressure; cook 5 minutes.
5 Release pressure using the quick release method (page 6); remove lid. Add peas; simmer, uncovered, until peas are tender and season to taste. Serve sprinkled with parsley.

prep + cook time 40 minutes **serves** 4
nutritional count per serving 21.9g total fat (8.3g saturated fat); 1994kJ (477 cal); 31.2g carbohydrate; 34g protein; 9.6g fibre

If you have an electric pressure cooker you won't need to reduce the heat to stabilise pressure, your cooker will automatically stabilise itself. Always check with the manufacturer's instructions before using. Recipe not suitable to freeze.

cassoulet

1½ cups (300g) dried white beans
500g (1 pound) boneless pork belly, rind on
1 dried bay leaf
1.25 litres (5 cups) water
2 tablespoons olive oil
4 toulouse sausages (480g)
4 lamb neck chops (680g), trimmed
150g (4½ ounces) speck, chopped finely
1 large brown onion (200g), chopped finely
4 cloves garlic, crushed
410g (13 ounces) canned diced tomatoes
2 tablespoons tomato paste
1 cup (70g) fresh breadcrumbs
2 tablespoons finely chopped fresh flat-leaf parsley
1 clove garlic, crushed, extra

1 Combine beans, pork, bay leaf and the water in 6-litre (24-cup) pressure cooker; secure lid. Bring cooker to high pressure. Reduce heat to stabilise pressure; cook 30 minutes.
2 Release pressure using the quick release method (page 6); remove lid. Strain pork mixture over large heatproof bowl. Discard bay leaf; reserve pork, beans and cooking liquid separately.
3 Heat half the oil in cooker; cook sausages until browned. Remove from cooker. Cook lamb in cooker until browned. Remove from cooker. Cook speck in cooker, stirring, until browned. Add onion and garlic; cook, stirring, until onion softens. Return lamb, sausages, pork and beans to cooker with undrained tomatoes, paste and 1½ cups (375ml) of the reserved cooking liquid; secure lid. Bring cooker to high pressure. Reduce heat to stabilise pressure; cook 20 minutes.

4 Release pressure using the quick release method (page 6); remove lid. Remove pork, lamb and sausages. Secure lid of cooker; bring cooker to high pressure. Reduce heat to stabilise pressure; cook 5 minutes.
5 Meanwhile, coarsely chop pork and sausages; discard bones from lamb, chop meat coarsely.
6 Release cooker pressure using quick release method (page 6); remove lid. Return meat to cooker; simmer, uncovered, until hot. Season to taste.
7 Heat remaining oil in medium frying pan; cook breadcrumbs, stirring, until browned and crisp. Stir in parsley and extra garlic. Transfer cassoulet to serving dish; sprinkle with breadcrumb mixture.

prep + cook time 1 hour 15 minutes serves 8
nutritional count per serving 44.1g total fat (15.8g saturated fat); 2913kJ (697 cal); 24.6g carbohydrate; 46.4g protein; 9.6g fibre

If you have an electric pressure cooker you won't need to reduce the heat to stabilise pressure, your cooker will automatically stabilise itself. Always check with the manufacturer's instructions before using. There are several versions of cassoulet, which originates from the south west of France. We used cannellini beans for this recipe but you can also use lima or haricot beans. Recipe suitable to freeze.

white wine and lamb one pot

2 tablespoons olive oil
800g (1½ pounds) boned lamb leg,
    chopped coarsely
1 large brown onion (200g), chopped finely
1 cup (250ml) dry white wine
600g (1¼ pounds) kipfler potatoes, peeled,
    chopped coarsely
2 cups (240g) frozen peas
3 eggs
½ cup (40g) finely grated parmesan cheese
⅓ cup coarsely chopped fresh flat-leaf parsley

1 Heat oil in 6-litre (24-cup) pressure cooker; cook lamb, in batches, until browned. Remove from cooker.
2 Cook onion in cooker, stirring, until soft. Return lamb to cooker with wine; secure lid. Bring cooker to high pressure. Reduce heat to stabilise pressure; cook 20 minutes.
3 Release pressure using the quick release method (page 6); remove lid. Add potato; secure lid. Bring cooker to high pressure. Reduce heat to stabilise pressure; cook 5 minutes.
4 Release pressure using the quick release method (page 6); remove lid. Add peas; simmer, uncovered, until peas are tender. Remove from heat.
5 Whisk eggs and cheese in medium bowl; stir into hot lamb mixture until sauce thickens. Season to taste. Serve sprinkled with parsley and extra grated parmesan cheese, if you like.

prep + cook time 45 minutes **serves** 4
nutritional count per serving 27.4g total fat
(9.4g saturated fat); 2571kJ (615 cal);
19.5g carbohydrate; 59.6g protein; 5.6g fibre

If you have an electric pressure cooker you won't need to reduce the heat to stabilise pressure, your cooker will automatically stabilise itself. Always check with the manufacturer's instructions before using. Thickening a sauce with eggs at the end of cooking is done in many European countries such as Italy and Greece. Recipe not suitable to freeze.

lamb rogan josh

2 tablespoons ghee
800g (1½ pounds) lamb neck chops, trimmed
2 large brown onions (400g), chopped finely
4 cloves garlic, crushed
½ cup (150g) rogan josh curry paste
410g (13 ounces) canned tomato puree
¼ cup (60ml) water
250g (8 ounces) spinach, trimmed,
  chopped coarsely
½ cup coarsely chopped fresh
  coriander (cilantro)

1 Heat half the ghee in 6-litre (24-cup) pressure
cooker; cook lamb, in batches, until browned.
Remove from cooker.
2 Heat remaining ghee in cooker; cook onion,
stirring, until browned lightly. Add garlic; cook,
stirring, until fragrant. Return lamb to cooker with
paste, puree and the water; secure lid. Bring cooker
to high pressure. Reduce heat to stabilise pressure;
cook 25 minutes.
3 Release pressure using the quick release
method (page 6); remove lid. Stir in spinach and
coriander; season to taste.

prep + cook time 45 minutes serves 4
nutritional count per serving 38.1g total fat
(12.2g saturated fat); 2378kJ (569 cal);
14.3g carbohydrate; 37.8g protein; 9.3g fibre

serving suggestion Serve with steamed basmati
rice, pappadums and raita.

If you have an electric pressure cooker you won't
need to reduce the heat to stabilise pressure,
your cooker will automatically stabilise itself.
Always check with the manufacturer's instructions
before using. Recipe suitable to freeze.

spicy lamb in tomato and spinach sauce

1 tablespoon vegetable oil
1kg (2 pounds) boned lamb leg, chopped coarsely
1 medium brown onion (150g), chopped finely
3 cloves garlic, crushed
2 fresh small red thai (serrano) chillies,
  chopped finely
2 teaspoons each ground coriander and
  garam masala
1 teaspoon each ground cumin and
  ground fenugreek
½ teaspoon ground turmeric
410g (13 ounces) canned crushed tomatoes
½ cup (125ml) beef stock
100g (3 ounces) baby spinach leaves, shredded finely
2 tablespoons finely chopped fresh
  coriander (cilantro)

1 Heat half the oil in 6-litre (24-cup) pressure cooker; cook lamb, in batches, until browned. Remove from cooker.
2 Heat remaining oil in cooker; cook onion, garlic and chilli, stirring, until onion softens. Add spices; cook, stirring, until fragrant. Return lamb to cooker with undrained tomatoes and stock; secure lid. Bring cooker to high pressure. Reduce heat to stabilise pressure; cook 25 minutes.
3 Release pressure using the quick release method (page 6); remove lid. Stir in spinach and coriander; season to taste.

prep + cook time 40 minutes **serves** 4
nutritional count per serving 18.5g total fat (6.6g saturated fat); 1789kJ (428 cal); 5.8g carbohydrate; 57.8g protein; 2.9g fibre

serving suggestion Serve with steamed basmati rice and warm naan.

If you have an electric pressure cooker you won't need to reduce the heat to stabilise pressure, your cooker will automatically stabilise itself. Always check with the manufacturer's instructions before using. Recipe suitable to freeze.

lemon and ginger lamb shanks with broad beans

1 tablespoon olive oil
4 french-trimmed lamb shanks (1kg)
1 large brown onion (200g), chopped finely
3 cloves garlic, crushed
2 tablespoons thinly sliced preserved lemon rind
5cm (2-inch) piece fresh ginger (25g), grated
1 cinnamon stick
¼ cup (60ml) lemon juice
½ cup (125ml) water
300g (9½ ounces) frozen broad beans (fava beans)
600g (1¼ pounds) kipfler potatoes, halved
20g (¾ ounce) butter
1 cup finely chopped fresh coriander (cilantro)
½ cup finely chopped fresh flat-leaf parsley

1 Heat half the oil in 6-litre (24-cup) pressure cooker; cook lamb, in batches, until browned. Remove from cooker.
2 Heat remaining oil in cooker; cook onion and garlic, stirring, until onion softens. Add preserved lemon, ginger and cinnamon; cook, stirring, until fragrant. Return lamb to cooker with juice and the water; secure lid. Bring cooker to high pressure. Reduce heat to stabilise pressure; cook 25 minutes.
3 Meanwhile, cook beans in large saucepan of boiling water about 2 minutes or until tender; drain. Rinse under cold water; drain. Peel away grey skins.
4 Release pressure using the quick release method (page 6); remove lid. Add potato; secure lid. Bring cooker to high pressure. Reduce heat to stabilise pressure; cook 10 minutes.
5 Meanwhile, melt butter in medium frying pan; cook herbs, stirring, until bright green.
6 Release cooker pressure using the quick release method (page 6); remove lid. Stir in beans and herbs; simmer, uncovered until hot. Season to taste.

prep + cook time 50 minutes **serves** 4
nutritional count per serving 21.5g total fat (9g saturated fat); 1952kJ (467 cal); 26.5g carbohydrate; 36.4g protein; 11.5g fibre

If you have an electric pressure cooker you won't need to reduce the heat to stabilise pressure, your cooker will automatically stabilise itself. Always check with the manufacturer's instructions before using. Preserved lemons, a prominent ingredient in North African cooking, are salted lemons bottled for several months; the flavour is salty, unique and perfumed. To use, discard flesh, rinse well, using rind only. This recipe is not suitable to freeze.

raan with rice pilau

1 teaspoon each ground coriander, cumin, cinnamon, turmeric and chilli powder
½ teaspoon ground cardamom
¼ teaspoon ground cloves
1 medium brown onion (150g), chopped coarsely
3 cloves garlic, quartered
2.5cm (1-inch) piece fresh ginger (15g), sliced thinly
¼ cup (35g) roasted slivered almonds
½ cup (140g) yogurt
2 tablespoons lemon juice
1.4kg (2¾-pound) easy-carve lamb leg
2 cups (500ml) water
1 tablespoon vegetable oil
1 medium brown onion (150g), chopped finely
1½ cups (300g) white long-grain rice
20g (¾ ounce) butter
2 teaspoons finely grated lemon rind
⅓ cup (45g) roasted slivered almonds, extra

1 Dry-fry spices in small frying pan, stirring, until fragrant. Remove from heat; cool. Blend or process spices, coarsely chopped onion, garlic, ginger, nuts, yogurt and juice until onion mixture forms a smooth paste.
2 Tie lamb leg, at 2cm (¾-inch) intervals, with kitchen string; rub paste all over lamb, season. Add the water to 8-litre (32-cup) pressure cooker. Place lamb on oiled wire rack in cooker; secure lid. Bring cooker to high pressure. Reduce heat to stabilise pressure; cook 30 minutes.

3 Release pressure using the quick release method (page 6); remove lid. Remove lamb from cooker; cover to keep warm. Strain cooking liquid; reserve 2¼ cups (560ml).
4 Heat oil in cooker; cook finely chopped onion, stirring, until soft. Add rice; stir to coat in onion mixture. Add reserved cooking liquid; secure lid. Bring cooker to high pressure. Reduce heat to stabilise pressure; cook 13 minutes.
5 Meanwhile, preheat grill (broiler). Place lamb on oven tray; grill about 10 minutes or until browned lightly.
6 Release cooker pressure using the quick release method (page 6); remove lid. Fluff rice with a fork; stir in butter, rind and extra nuts. Season to taste. Serve lamb with rice.

prep + cook time 1 hour serves 6
nutritional count per serving 23.6g total fat (7.4g saturated fat); 2429kJ (581 cal); 44.4g carbohydrate; 46.1g protein; 2.6g fibre

serving suggestion Serve raan with yogurt; sprinkle with coarsely chopped fresh coriander.

If you have an electric pressure cooker you won't need to reduce the heat to stabilise pressure, your cooker will automatically stabilise itself. Always check with the manufacturer's instructions before using. Recipe not suitable to freeze.

braised lamb shoulder with borlotti beans

1½ cups (300g) dried borlotti beans
700g (1½-pound) boned lamb shoulder
2 tablespoons olive oil
2 medium brown onions (300g), chopped finely
2 stalks celery (300g), trimmed, chopped finely
1 large carrot (180g), chopped finely
2 cloves garlic, crushed
410g (13 ounces) canned diced tomatoes
2 sprigs fresh rosemary
2 cups (500ml) water

1 Place beans in large bowl, cover with cold water; stand overnight. Rinse under cold water; drain.
2 Roll lamb tightly; tie with kitchen string, at 2cm (¾-inch) intervals, to secure. Season lamb. Heat half the oil in 6-litre (24-cup) pressure cooker; cook lamb until browned all over. Remove from cooker.
3 Add remaining oil to cooker; cook onion, celery and carrot, stirring, until vegetables soften. Add garlic; cook, stirring, until fragrant. Stir in beans, undrained tomatoes, rosemary and the water. Return lamb to cooker; secure lid. Bring cooker to high pressure. Reduce heat to stabilise pressure; cook 25 minutes.
4 Release pressure using the quick release method (page 6); remove lid. Remove lamb, cover loosely; stand 5 minutes. Secure lid of cooker; bring cooker to high pressure. Reduce heat to stabilise pressure; cook 5 minutes. Release pressure using the quick release method (page 6); remove lid. Discard rosemary; season to taste. Serve sliced lamb with bean mixture.

prep + cook time 50 minutes (+ standing) serves 4
nutritional count per serving 26.4g total fat (8.6g saturated fat); 2667kJ (638 cal); 36.7g carbohydrate; 53.2g protein; 20.6g fibre

serving suggestion Serve with crusty bread.

If you have an electric pressure cooker you won't need to reduce the heat to stabilise pressure, your cooker will automatically stabilise itself. Always check with the manufacturer's instructions before using. Recipe not suitable to freeze.

lamb and macadamia curry

1 tablespoon vegetable oil
1.2kg (2½ pounds) boned lamb leg,
  chopped coarsely
1 medium brown onion (150g), chopped finely
2 cloves garlic, crushed
1 fresh long red chilli, chopped finely
2 teaspoons garam masala
410g (13 ounces) canned crushed tomatoes
⅔ cup (160ml) coconut milk
1 cup (120g) ground macadamias
⅓ cup (45g) coarsely chopped, roasted
  unsalted macadamias
⅓ cup loosely packed fresh coriander (cilantro)

1 Heat half the oil in 6-litre (24-cup) pressure
cooker; cook lamb, in batches, until browned.
Remove from cooker.
2 Heat remaining oil in cooker; cook onion, garlic
and chilli, stirring, until onion softens. Add spice;
cook, stirring, until fragrant. Return lamb to cooker
with undrained tomatoes and coconut milk; secure
lid. Bring cooker to high pressure. Reduce heat to
stabilise pressure; cook 25 minutes.
3 Release pressure using the quick release
method (page 6); remove lid. Stir in ground nuts;
season to taste. Serve curry sprinkled with chopped
nuts and coriander.

prep + cook time 35 minutes **serves** 6
nutritional count per serving 39.3g total fat
(12.7g saturated fat); 2387kJ (571 cal);
5.8g carbohydrate; 47.7g protein; 3.5g fibre

If you have an electric pressure cooker you won't
need to reduce the heat to stabilise pressure,
your cooker will automatically stabilise itself.
Always check with the manufacturer's instructions
before using. You will need to blend or process
120g (4 ounces) roasted unsalted macadamia nuts
for enough ground nuts for this recipe. Recipe not
suitable to freeze.

lamb and apricot tagine

1 tablespoon olive oil
1kg (2 pounds) boned lamb shoulder, trimmed, chopped coarsely
1 medium brown onion (150g), sliced thinly
2 cloves garlic, crushed
1 teaspoon each ground cumin, coriander and cinnamon
¾ cup (180ml) beef stock
½ cup (75g) coarsely chopped dried apricots
100g (3 ounces) baby spinach leaves
¼ cup (35g) roasted slivered almonds

1   Heat half the oil in 6-litre (24-cup) pressure cooker; cook lamb, in batches, until browned. Remove from cooker.
2   Heat remaining oil in cooker; cook onion and garlic, stirring, until onion softens. Add spices; cook, stirring, until fragrant. Return lamb to cooker with stock; secure lid. Bring cooker to high pressure. Reduce heat to stabilise pressure; cook 25 minutes.
3   Release pressure using the quick release method (page 6); remove lid. Add apricots; secure lid. Bring cooker to high pressure. Reduce heat to stabilise pressure; cook 2 minutes. Release pressure using the quick release method (page 6); remove lid. Stir in spinach; season to taste. Serve tagine sprinkled with nuts.

prep + cook time 40 minutes **serves** 6
nutritional count per serving 21.3g total fat (7.5g saturated fat); 1526kJ (365 cal); 7.2g carbohydrate; 35g protein; 2.6g fibre

serving suggestion Serve with couscous.

If you have an electric pressure cooker you won't need to reduce the heat to stabilise pressure, your cooker will automatically stabilise itself. Always check with the manufacturer's instructions before using. Recipe suitable to freeze.

hot-peppered lamb curry

2 fresh long green chillies
2 tablespoons ghee
600g (1¼ pounds) boned lamb leg,
  chopped coarsely
2 large brown onions (400g), sliced thinly
3 cloves garlic, crushed
4cm (1½-inch) piece fresh ginger (20g), grated
3 cloves
4 green cardamom pods, bruised
2 cinnamon sticks
2 teaspoons coarsely cracked black pepper
2 medium tomatoes (300g), chopped finely
¼ cup (70g) yogurt
½ cup (125ml) water
¼ cup (60ml) lemon juice
⅓ cup finely chopped fresh coriander (cilantro)

1 Finely chop 1 of the chillies; finely shred remaining chilli.
2 Heat half the ghee in 6-litre (24-cup) pressure cooker; cook lamb, in batches, until browned. Remove from cooker.
3 Heat remaining ghee in same cooker; cook onion, stirring, about 5 minutes or until browned lightly. Add garlic and ginger; cook, stirring, until fragrant. Return lamb to cooker with spices, tomato, chopped chilli, yogurt and the water; secure lid. Bring cooker to high pressure. Reduce heat to stabilise pressure; cook 25 minutes.
4 Release pressure using the quick release method (page 6); remove lid. Stir in juice; season to taste. Serve sprinkled with coriander and shredded chilli, if you like.

prep + cook time 1 hour **serves** 4
nutritional count per serving 17.7g total fat (9.7g saturated fat); 1442kJ (345 cal); 8.6g carbohydrate; 36.5g protein; 3g fibre

serving suggestion Serve with steamed white long-grain rice.

If you have an electric pressure cooker you won't need to reduce the heat to stabilise pressure, your cooker will automatically stabilise itself. Always check with the manufacturer's instructions before using. This is a hot curry. If you prefer a milder version, reduce the amount of pepper and chilli. You can also serve it with an extra dollop of yogurt if you like. Recipe suitable to freeze.

braised lamb shanks with mushroom risotto

2 tablespoons olive oil
6 french-trimmed lamb shanks (1.5kg)
3 stalks celery (450g), untrimmed, halved
1 medium leek (350g), trimmed, halved
3 stalks fresh rosemary
3 cloves garlic, bruised
1 litre (4 cups) water
⅔ cup (20g) mixed dried mushrooms
1 large brown onion (200g), chopped finely
1½ cups (300g) arborio rice
½ cup (125ml) dry white wine
½ cup (40g) finely grated parmesan cheese
30g (1 ounce) butter, chopped finely

1 Heat half the oil in 6-litre (24-cup) pressure cooker; cook lamb, in batches, until browned. Remove from cooker.
2 Return lamb to cooker with celery, leek, rosemary, garlic and the water; secure lid. Bring cooker to high pressure. Reduce heat to stabilise pressure; cook 30 minutes.
3 Release pressure using the quick release method (page 6); remove lid. Strain over large heatproof bowl; cover shanks to keep warm. Discard vegetables. Reserve 3½ cups (875ml) cooking liquid; add dried mushrooms.
4 Heat remaining oil in cooker; cook onion, stirring, until soft. Add rice; stir to coat in onion mixture. Stir in wine and cooking liquid with mushrooms; secure lid. Bring cooker to high pressure. Reduce heat to stabilise pressure; cook 7 minutes.
5 Release pressure using the quick release method (page 6); remove lid. Stand, covered, 5 minutes or until liquid is absorbed. Stir in cheese and butter; season to taste. Sprinkle risotto with a little extra rosemary and grated parmesan; serve with shanks.

prep + cook time 50 minutes serves 6
nutritional count per serving 25.1g total fat (10.6g saturated fat); 2353kJ (563 cal); 43.8g carbohydrate; 35.5g protein; 3.1g fibre

If you have an electric pressure cooker you won't need to reduce the heat to stabilise pressure, your cooker will automatically stabilise itself. Always check with the manufacturer's instructions before using. Covering the shanks with the cooked celery and leek is an easy way to keep the lamb hot and moist while you cook the risotto. Recipe not suitable to freeze.

pork

maple syrup pork stew

1 tablespoon olive oil
1kg (2 pounds) pork neck, chopped coarsely
1 medium brown onion (150g), chopped finely
2 cloves garlic, crushed
¼ cup (60ml) maple syrup
¼ cup (60ml) orange juice
½ cup (125ml) chicken stock
280g (9 ounces) baby carrots, trimmed
2 celery stalks (300g), trimmed, cut into
  thick matchsticks
2 tablespoons dried currants
100g (3 ounces) baby spinach leaves

1 Heat half the oil in 6-litre (24-cup) pressure cooker; cook pork, in batches, until browned. Remove from cooker.
2 Heat remaining oil in cooker; cook onion and garlic, stirring, until onion softens. Return pork to cooker with syrup, juice and stock; secure lid. Bring cooker to high pressure. Reduce heat to stabilise pressure; cook 20 minutes.
3 Release pressure using the quick release method (page 6); remove lid. Add carrots, celery and currants; secure lid. Bring cooker to high pressure. Reduce heat to stabilise pressure; cook 5 minutes.
4 Release pressure using the quick release method (page 6); remove lid. Stir in spinach; season to taste.

prep + cook time 35 minutes **serves** 4
nutritional count per serving 25g total fat
(7.5g saturated fat); 2328kJ (557 cal);
25g carbohydrate; 55.5g protein; 4.7g fibre

If you have an electric pressure cooker you won't need to reduce the heat to stabilise pressure, your cooker will automatically stabilise itself. Always check with the manufacturer's instructions before using. Recipe suitable to freeze.

best-ever bolognese sauce

1 tablespoon olive oil
1 medium brown onion (150g), chopped finely
2 cloves garlic, crushed
750g (1½ pounds) minced (ground) pork and veal
⅓ cup (95g) tomato paste
800g (1½ pounds) canned crushed tomatoes
½ cup (125ml) dry red wine
2 tablespoons each finely chopped fresh flat-leaf
  parsley and oregano

1 Heat oil in 6-litre (24-cup) pressure cooker; add onion and garlic; cook, stirring, until onion softens. Add pork and veal; cook, stirring, until browned. Add paste, undrained tomatoes and wine to cooker; secure lid. Bring cooker to high pressure. Reduce heat to stabilise pressure; cook 20 minutes.
2 Release pressure using the quick release method (page 6); remove lid. Simmer, uncovered, about 10 minutes or until sauce thickens slightly. Stir in herbs; season to taste.

prep + cook time 45 minutes **makes** 6 cups
nutritional count per 1 cup 12.2g total fat
(3.8g saturated fat); 1129kJ (270 cal);
7.2g carbohydrate; 28.2g protein; 2.8g fibre

serving suggestion Cook 500g dry spaghetti for enough pasta to serve with this sauce. Leftover sauce can be used to make lasagne or served over roasted jacket potatoes.

If you have an electric pressure cooker you won't need to reduce the heat to stabilise pressure, your cooker will automatically stabilise itself. Always check with the manufacturer's instructions before using. Recipe suitable to freeze.

pickled pork

1.5kg (3-pound) piece boneless rolled shoulder
  of pickled pork
2 dried bay leaves
8 black peppercorns
4 whole cloves
1 medium brown onion (150g), chopped coarsely
1 celery stalk (150g), trimmed, chopped coarsely
2 tablespoons light brown sugar
2 tablespoons malt vinegar
3 litres (12 cups) water, approximately

1   Combine pork, bay leaves, peppercorns, cloves,
onion, celery, sugar, vinegar and enough of the
water to barely cover pork in 8-litre (32-cup)
pressure cooker; secure lid. Bring cooker to high
pressure. Reduce heat to stabilise pressure; cook
30 minutes.
2   Release pressure using the quick release
method (page 6); remove lid. Cool pork, covered
loosely in cooking liquid. Serve warm or cold.

prep + cook time 35 minutes (+ cooling) **serves** 6
nutritional count per serving 18.8g total fat
(7.3g saturated fat); 1956kJ (468 cal);
5.7g carbohydrate; 68.5g protein; 0.6g fibre

serving suggestion Serve warm with creamy
mashed potatoes and a salad or steamed vegies.
Or cover and refrigerate overnight to make
wonderful sandwiches – don't forget the mustard
or a favourite pickle, chutney or relish.

If you have an electric pressure cooker you won't
need to reduce the heat to stabilise pressure,
your cooker will automatically stabilise itself.
Always check with the manufacturer's instructions
before using. Pickled pork is a little old-fashioned,
it might be necessary to order it from the butcher.
The shoulder cut used here is also called a "hand"
of pickled pork. Recipe suitable to freeze.

Feijoada is traditionally a Portuguese dish made with red kidney beans. Its name comes from "feijõa", Portuguese for beans. Imported to Brazil (a former Portuguese colony), feijoada, pronounced "fey-ju-arda" has become over time their national dish. It usually contains pigs' ears and trotters and is served sprinkled with farofa (roasted cassava flour).

brazilian feijoada

600g (1¼ pounds) boneless pork belly, rind on
600g (1¼ pounds) american-style pork spare ribs
2 cups (400g) dried black (turtle) beans
2 dried bay leaves
1.5 litres (6 cups) water
2 tablespoons olive oil
150g (4½ ounces) speck, chopped finely
1 large brown onion (200g), chopped finely
5 cloves garlic, crushed
1 cured chorizo sausage (170g)
2 tablespoons coarsely chopped flat-leaf parsley

1 Chop pork belly coarsely, cut ribs into serving sized pieces.
2 Combine beans, pork belly, ribs, bay leaves and the water in 6-litre (24-cup) pressure cooker; secure lid. Bring cooker to high pressure. Reduce heat to stabilise pressure; cook 35 minutes.
3 Release pressure using the quick release method (page 6); remove lid. Strain over large heatproof bowl. Reserve 2 cups (500ml) cooking liquid; reserve bay leaves.

4 Heat oil in cooker; cook speck and reserved bay leaves, stirring, until speck is browned. Add onion and garlic; cook, stirring, until onion softens. Return beans, pork belly and ribs to cooker with whole chorizo and reserved cooking liquid; secure lid. Bring cooker to high pressure. Reduce heat to stabilise pressure; cook 10 minutes.
5 Release pressure using the quick release method (page 6); remove lid. Remove chorizo; chop coarsely, return to cooker. Season to taste. Serve sprinkled with parsley

prep + cook time 1 hour serves 8
nutritional count per serving 41.8g total fat (11.7g saturated fat); 2529kJ (605 cal); 7.4g carbohydrate; 45.5g protein; 11.2g fibre

serving suggestion Serve with steamed rice.

If you have an electric pressure cooker you won't need to reduce the heat to stabilise pressure, your cooker will automatically stabilise itself. Always check with the manufacturer's instructions before using. Recipe suitable to freeze.

ham hock with lentils

1 ham hock (1kg)
1 dried bay leaf
1 litre (4 cups) water
2 tablespoons olive oil
1 large brown onion (200g), chopped finely
2 cloves garlic, crushed
2 tablespoons tomato paste
1 medium (120g) carrot, chopped coarsely
1½ cups (300g) french-style green lentils
⅓ cup coarsely chopped fresh flat-leaf parsley

1 Combine ham, bay leaf and the water in 6-litre (24-cup) pressure cooker; secure lid. Bring cooker to high pressure. Reduce heat to stabilise pressure; cook 15 minutes.
2 Release pressure using the quick release method (page 6); remove lid. Strain mixture over large heatproof bowl. Reserve ham and 3 cups (750ml) cooking liquid; discard bay leaf.
3 Heat oil in cooker; add onion and garlic, cook, stirring, until onion softens. Return ham to cooker with reserved cooking liquid, paste, carrot and lentils; secure lid. Bring cooker to high pressure. Reduce heat to stabilise pressure; cook 15 minutes.
4 Release pressure using the quick release method (page 6); remove lid, season to taste. Remove ham from cooker. When cool enough to handle remove ham from bone, chop ham coarsely; discard skin, fat and bone. Return ham to cooker, reheat before serving. Sprinkle with parsley.

prep + cook time 35 minutes serves 4
nutritional count per serving 21.9g total fat (5.6g saturated fat); 2349kJ (562 cal); 33.8g carbohydrate; 53.3g protein; 12.6g fibre

serving suggestion Serve this dish with a salad of baby spinach.

If you have an electric pressure cooker you won't need to reduce the heat to stabilise pressure, your cooker will automatically stabilise itself. Always check with the manufacturer's instructions before using. Recipe not suitable to freeze.

sticky pork spare ribs

1.5kg (3 pounds) american-style pork spare ribs
1 cup (250ml) water
⅓ cup (115g) orange marmalade
⅓ cup (80ml) kecap manis
4 cloves garlic, crushed
8cm (3-inch) piece fresh ginger (40g), grated
2 teaspoons five-spice powder

1 Combine ribs and the water in 6-litre (24-cup) pressure cooker; secure lid. Bring cooker to high pressure. Reduce heat to stabilise pressure; cook 15 minutes.
2 Meanwhile, combine remaining ingredients in large bowl. Preheat grill (broiler).
3 Release cooker pressure using the quick release method (page 6); remove lid. Drain ribs; combine with marmalade mixture. Place ribs, in single layer, on oiled wire rack over large shallow baking dish filled with 1cm (½ inch) water. Grill ribs about 8 minutes or until browned, turning halfway through cooking time and brushing occasionally with remaining marmalade mixture.

prep + cook time 20 minutes **serves** 4
nutritional count per serving 13.6g total fat (4.6g saturated fat); 1484kJ (355 cal); 20.2g carbohydrate; 37.2g protein; 1g fibre

If you have an electric pressure cooker you won't need to reduce the heat to stabilise pressure, your cooker will automatically stabilise itself. Always check with the manufacturer's instructions before using. Recipe not suitable to freeze.

caramelised pepper pork

3 shallots (75g), chopped finely
2 cloves garlic, crushed
2 tablespoons fish sauce
1 tablespoon coarsely cracked black pepper
800g (1½ pounds) boneless pork belly, rind
  removed, chopped coarsely
1 tablespoon peanut oil
2 tablespoons dark brown sugar
⅓ cup (80ml) water
2 green onions (scallions), sliced finely

1 Combine shallot, garlic, sauce, pepper and pork
in large bowl.
2 Heat oil in 6-litre (24-cup) pressure cooker; cook
pork, in batches, until browned. Remove from cooker.
3 Return pork to cooker with sugar; cook, stirring,
until sugar caramelises. Add the water; secure lid.
Bring cooker to high pressure. Reduce heat to
stabilise pressure; cook 20 minutes.
4 Release pressure using the quick release method
(page 6); remove lid. Serve sprinkled with onion.

prep + cook time 35 minutes **serves** 4
nutritional count per serving 43g total fat
(13.9g saturated fat); 2270kJ (543 cal);
7.5g carbohydrate; 32.3g protein; 0.6g fibre

serving suggestion Serve with steamed rice.

If you have an electric pressure cooker you won't
need to reduce the heat to stabilise pressure,
your cooker will automatically stabilise itself.
Always check with the manufacturer's instructions
before using. Recipe suitable to freeze.

pork and fennel sausage risotto

6 pork and fennel sausages (380g)
1 tablespoon olive oil
20g (¾ ounce) butter
1 medium brown onion (150g), chopped finely
1 medium fennel bulb (300g), trimmed,
   chopped finely
1 clove garlic, crushed
1½ cups (300g) arborio rice
½ cup (125ml) dry white wine
3½ cups (875ml) chicken stock
2 cups (500ml) water
½ cup (60g) frozen peas
½ cup (40g) finely grated parmesan cheese
2 teaspoons finely chopped fresh thyme

1 Cook sausages in heated 6-litre (24-cup) pressure cooker until browned. Remove from cooker; slice thinly.
2 Heat oil and butter in cooker; cook onion, fennel and garlic, stirring, until vegetables soften. Add rice; stir to coat in butter mixture. Add wine; simmer, uncovered, until liquid is absorbed. Add stock and the water; secure lid. Bring cooker to high pressure. Reduce heat to stabilise pressure; cook 7 minutes.
3 Release pressure using the quick release method (page 6); remove lid. Add sausage and peas; cover, stand 5 minutes. Stir in half the cheese and thyme; season to taste.
4 Serve risotto sprinkled with remaining cheese.

prep + cook time 25 minutes serves 4
nutritional count per serving 34.4g total fat (14.5g saturated fat); 2964kJ (709 cal); 68.3g carbohydrate; 24.6g protein; 4.5g fibre

If you have an electric pressure cooker you won't need to reduce the heat to stabilise pressure, your cooker will automatically stabilise itself. Always check with the manufacturer's instructions before using. Recipe not suitable to freeze.

hoisin pork with salted crackling

1.2kg (2½ pounds) boneless pork belly, rind on
1 cinnamon stick
2 star anise
⅓ cup (120g) hoisin sauce
5cm (2 inch) strip orange rind
½ cup (125ml) orange juice
½ cup (125ml) water
1 tablespoon fine cooking salt
1 bunch choy sum, trimmed

1 Using small sharp knife, score pork rind at shallow 1cm (½-inch) intervals.
2 Combine cinnamon, star anise, sauce, rind, juice and the water in 6-litre (24-cup) pressure cooker. Place pork, rind-side up, on oiled wire rack in cooker; secure lid. Bring cooker to high pressure. Reduce heat to stabilise pressure; cook 30 minutes.
3 Release pressure using the quick release method (page 6); remove lid. Remove pork from cooker; strain cooking liquid into small saucepan.
4 Place pork, rind-side up, on wire rack over large shallow baking dish; sprinkle rind with salt. Preheat griller (broiler). Grill pork about 10 minutes or until crackling is browned lightly and crisp.
5 Meanwhile, bring reserved cooking liquid to the boil. Boil, uncovered, about 5 minutes or until sauce thickens slightly. Add choy sum, cook until wilted.
6 Cut pork into six pieces. Serve pork with sauce and choy sum.

prep + cook time 45 minutes **serves** 6
nutritional count per serving 45.9g total fat (15.4g saturated fat); 2521kJ (603 cal); 9.9g carbohydrate; 37.6g protein; 3.2g fibre

If you have an electric pressure cooker you won't need to reduce the heat to stabilise pressure, your cooker will automatically stabilise itself. Always check with the manufacturer's instructions before using. Recipe not suitable to freeze.

hungarian pork cabbage rolls

410g (13 ounces) canned sauerkraut
10 large cabbage leaves (500g)
1 tablespoon olive oil
50g (1½ ounces) speck, chopped finely
1 large brown onion (200g), chopped finely
3 cloves garlic, crushed
300g (9½ ounces) minced (ground) pork
½ cup (100g) long-grain white rice
2 teaspoons smoked paprika
1 teaspoon ground allspice
410g (13 ounces) canned tomato puree
1 cup (250ml) water
¼ cup (60g) sour cream

1 Drain sauerkraut; place in large bowl. Cover sauerkraut with cold water, stand 15 minutes; drain. Rinse under cold water; drain.
2 Meanwhile, trim large stems from cabbage leaves. Boil, steam or microwave leaves until pliable; drain. Rinse under cold water; drain. Pat dry with absorbent paper.
3 Heat oil in 6-litre (24-cup) pressure cooker; cook speck, onion and garlic, stirring, until onion softens. Remove from cooker; cool.
4 Combine onion mixture, pork, rice and spices in medium bowl; season.

5 Place one cabbage leaf, vein-side up, on board; cut leaf in half lengthways. Place heaped tablespoons of pork mixture at stem end of each piece of cabbage; roll cabbage tightly over filling, fold in sides. Continue rolling to enclose filling. Repeat with remaining cabbage and pork mixture.
6 Place sauerkraut in cooker; top with cabbage rolls, seam-side down. Combine puree and the water; pour over rolls. Secure lid; bring cooker to high pressure. Reduce heat to stabilise pressure; cook 10 minutes.
7 Release pressure using the quick release method (page 6); remove lid. Remove rolls from cooker. Stir sour cream into sauerkraut mixture; simmer, uncovered, until hot, season to taste. Serve sauerkraut topped with rolls.

prep + cook time 50 minutes (+ standing)
makes 12
nutritional count per roll 6.1g total fat (2.4g saturated fat); 577kJ (138 cal); 10.9g carbohydrate; 8.4g protein; 3.5g fibre

If you have an electric pressure cooker you won't need to reduce the heat to stabilise pressure, your cooker will automatically stabilise itself. Always check with the manufacturer's instructions before using. Recipe not suitable to freeze.

italian chilli braised pork

800g (1½ pounds) boned pork shoulder
2 tablespoons olive oil
4 cloves garlic, crushed
4 drained anchovy fillets, chopped finely
410g (13 ounces) canned diced tomatoes
¼ cup (60ml) water
2 tablespoons finely chopped fresh oregano
1 tablespoon rinsed drained baby capers
½ teaspoon dried chilli flakes
½ cup (75g) seeded kalamata olives

1 Roll pork tightly; tie with kitchen string, at 2cm (¾-inch) intervals, to secure. Season pork. Heat half the oil in 6-litre (24-cup) pressure cooker; cook pork until browned all over. Remove from cooker.
2 Heat remaining oil in cooker; cook garlic and anchovy, stirring, until fragrant. Stir in undrained tomatoes, the water, oregano, capers and chilli. Return pork to cooker; secure lid. Bring cooker to high pressure. Reduce heat to stabilise pressure; cook 25 minutes.
3 Release pressure using the quick release method (page 6); remove lid. Remove pork, cover; stand 5 minutes then slice thinly. Stir olives into sauce; season to taste. Serve pork with sauce. Sprinkle with some extra oregano if you like

prep + cook time 30 minutes **serves** 4
nutritional count per serving 26g total fat (6.8g saturated fat); 1868kJ (447 cal); 8.1g carbohydrate; 44.6g protein; 2g fibre

serving suggestion Serve with creamy polenta.

If you have an electric pressure cooker you won't need to reduce the heat to stabilise pressure, your cooker will automatically stabilise itself. Always check with the manufacturer's instructions before using. If cooked slightly pink, pork is very tender and moist. If you prefer it well done, cook it for 2 minutes longer. Recipe not suitable to freeze.

pork, fennel and olive ragout

2 tablespoons plain (all-purpose) flour
1kg (2 pounds) pork neck, chopped coarsely
1 tablespoon olive oil
1 medium leek (350g), sliced thinly
1 medium fennel bulb (300g), trimmed,
  sliced thinly
2 cloves garlic, crushed
⅓ cup (80ml) dry white wine
½ cup (125ml) chicken stock
2 tablespoons white balsamic vinegar
½ cup (60g) seeded mixed olives
2 tablespoons coarsely chopped fresh
  flat-leaf parsley

1   Season flour in large bowl; add pork, toss to
coat in flour. Shake off excess. Heat half the oil in
6-litre (24-cup) pressure cooker; cook pork, in
batches, until browned. Remove from cooker.
2   Heat remaining oil in cooker; cook leek, fennel
and garlic, stirring, until vegetables soften. Return
pork to cooker with wine, stock and vinegar; secure
lid. Bring cooker to high pressure. Reduce heat to
stabilise pressure; cook 30 minutes.
3   Release pressure using the quick release method
(page 6); remove lid. Stir in olives; season to taste.
Serve ragout sprinkled with parsley.

prep + cook time 45 minutes **serves** 4
nutritional count per serving 25.2g total fat
(7.5g saturated fat); 2149kJ (514 cal);
11.2g carbohydrate; 55.7g protein; 3.4g fibre

If you have an electric pressure cooker you won't
need to reduce the heat to stabilise pressure,
your cooker will automatically stabilise itself.
Always check with the manufacturer's instructions
before using. Recipe suitable to freeze.

desserts

maple syrup and date puddings

⅔ cup (90g) dried seedless dates
⅔ cup (160ml) boiling water
½ teaspoon bicarbonate of soda (baking soda)
45g (1½ ounces) butter
⅓ cup (75g) firmly packed light brown sugar
1 tablespoon maple syrup
1 egg
1 egg yolk
⅔ cup (100g) self-raising flour
⅓ cup (50g) plain (all-purpose) flour

MAPLE SAUCE
2 tablespoons maple syrup
1 tablespoon light brown sugar
2 tablespoons water
20g (¾ ounce) butter

1 Grease four 1-cup (250ml) ovenproof dishes.
2 Combine dates, the water and soda in food processor bowl; stand 5 minutes. Process date mixture until smooth. Add butter, sugar, syrup, egg and yolk; process until combined. Add sifted flours; process until combined.
3 Divide mixture among dishes; cover tightly with foil. Place 1½ cups (375ml) water in 8-litre (32-cup) pressure cooker. Place dishes into cooker; secure lid of cooker. Bring cooker to high pressure. Reduce heat to stabilise pressure; cook 10 minutes.
4 Meanwhile, make maple sauce.
5 Release cooker pressure using the quick release method (page 6); remove lid. Remove dishes from cooker. Turn puddings onto serving plates; serve drizzled with sauce.

MAPLE SAUCE Combine ingredients in small saucepan; stir over heat, without boiling, until sugar dissolves. Bring to the boil; reduce heat. Simmer, uncovered, about 4 minutes or until thickened slightly.

prep + cook time 40 minutes serves 4
nutritional count per serving 16.6g total fat
(9.7g saturated fat); 2057kJ (492 cal);
76.6g carbohydrate; 6.8g protein; 3.6g fibre

If you have an electric pressure cooker you won't need to reduce the heat to stabilise pressure, your cooker will automatically stabilise itself. Always check with the manufacturer's instructions before using. Recipe not suitable to freeze.

lemon delicious

75g (2½ ounces) butter, melted
2 teaspoons finely grated lemon rind
1 cup (220g) caster (superfine) sugar
2 eggs, separated
½ cup (75g) self-raising flour
¼ cup (60ml) lemon juice
¾ cup (180ml) milk
2 teaspoons icing (confectioners') sugar

1 Grease 1.25-litre (5-cup), 16cm (6¼-inch) round
ovenproof dish.
2 Combine butter, rind, sugar and yolks in
medium bowl. Whisk in sifted flour then juice.
Gradually whisk in milk; mixture should be smooth
and runny.
3 Beat egg whites in small bowl with electric mixer
until soft peaks form; fold into lemon mixture in
two batches.
4 Spoon lemon mixture into dish; cover tightly
with foil. Place steamer basket in 6-litre (24-cup)
pressure cooker; add 1½ cups (375ml) water. Place
dish on a tea towel; use tea towel to lower dish into
basket in cooker. Fold tea towel overhang over top
of dish; secure lid of cooker. Bring cooker to high
pressure. Reduce heat to stabilise pressure; cook
27 minutes.
5 Release pressure using the quick release
method (page 6); remove lid. Remove dish from
cooker, dust lemon delicious with sifted icing sugar;
serve immediately.

prep + cook time 45 minutes **serves** 4
nutritional count per serving 20g total fat
(12.1g saturated fat); 2069kJ (495 cal);
71.1g carbohydrate; 6.9g protein; 0.8g fibre

If you have an electric pressure cooker you won't
need to reduce the heat to stabilise pressure,
your cooker will automatically stabilise itself.
Always check with the manufacturer's instructions
before using. Recipe not suitable to freeze.

vanilla rice pudding

¾ cup (150g) arborio rice
2½ cups (625ml) milk
1¼ cups (310ml) water
⅓ cup (75g) caster (superfine) sugar
20g (¾ ounce) butter
1 vanilla bean
¼ cup (55g) firmly packed light brown sugar

1 Combine rice, milk, the water, caster sugar and butter in 6-litre (24-cup) pressure cooker. Halve vanilla bean lengthways; scrape seeds into cooker, add vanilla bean. Secure lid of cooker. Bring cooker to high pressure. Reduce heat to stabilise pressure; cook 8 minutes.
2 Release pressure using the quick release method (page 6); remove lid. Stir pudding; stand 5 minutes. Discard vanilla bean. Serve pudding sprinkled with brown sugar.

prep + cook time 15 minutes **serves** 6
nutritional count per serving 6.9g total fat (4.5g saturated fat); 1104kJ (264 cal); 46.2g carbohydrate; 5.2g protein; 0.2g fibre

serving suggestion Serve with pouring cream or vanilla ice-cream.

If you have an electric pressure cooker you won't need to reduce the heat to stabilise pressure, your cooker will automatically stabilise itself. Always check with the manufacturer's instructions before using. Recipe not suitable to freeze.

steamed plum pudding

2 cups (300g) chopped mixed dried fruit
½ cup (75g) finely chopped dried seedless dates
½ cup (85g) finely chopped raisins
½ cup (125ml) water
¾ cup (165g) firmly packed light brown sugar
75g (2½ ounces) butter, chopped coarsely
½ teaspoon bicarbonate of soda (baking soda)
2 eggs, beaten lightly
¾ cup (110g) plain (all-purpose) flour
½ cup (75g) self-raising flour
1 teaspoon mixed spice
½ teaspoon ground cinnamon
2 tablespoons dark rum

1 Wash combined fruit under cold water; drain. Combine fruit, the water, sugar and butter in medium saucepan. Stir over heat until butter melts and sugar dissolves; bring to the boil. Reduce heat; simmer, uncovered, 5 minutes. Transfer mixture to large heatproof bowl, stir in soda; cool.
2 Stir eggs, sifted dry ingredients and rum into the fruit mixture.
3 Grease 1.25-litre (5-cup) pudding steamer; spoon mixture into steamer. Top with pleated baking paper and foil; secure with kitchen string or steamer lid.
4 Place steamer basket in 8-litre (32-cup) pressure cooker; add 2 cups (500ml) water. Place pudding steamer on a tea towel; use tea towel to lower steamer into basket in cooker. Fold tea towel overhang over top of steamer; secure lid of cooker. Bring cooker to high pressure. Reduce heat to stabilise pressure; cook 1 hour 10 minutes.
5 Release pressure using the quick release method (page 6); remove lid. Remove steamer from cooker; stand 10 minutes before turning out.

prep + cook time 1 hour 25 minutes (+ cooling)
serves 8
nutritional count per serving 9.7g total fat (5.7g saturated fat); 1806kJ (432 cal); 75.3g carbohydrate; 5.4g protein; 4.5g fibre

serving suggestion Serve with custard, brandy butter, cream or ice-cream.

If you have an electric pressure cooker you won't need to reduce the heat to stabilise pressure, your cooker will automatically stabilise itself. Always check with the manufacturer's instructions before using. Recipe suitable to freeze.

glossary

ALLSPICE also called pimento or jamaican pepper; tastes of nutmeg, cumin, clove and cinnamon. Available whole or ground.

ALMONDS
blanched brown skins removed.
flaked paper-thin slices.
meal also known as ground almonds.
slivered small pieces cut lengthways.

BARLEY a nutritious grain used in soups and stews. Hulled barley, the least processed, is high in fibre. Pearl barley has had the husk removed then been steamed and polished so that only the "pearl" of the grain remains.

BASIL
sweet the most common type of basil; used extensively in Italian dishes and a major ingredient in pesto.
thai also known as horapa; different from holy basil and sweet basil in both look and taste, with smaller leaves and purplish stems and an aniseed taste.

BAY LEAVES aromatic leaves from the bay tree available fresh or dried; adds a peppery flavour.

BEANS
black also called turtle beans or black kidney beans; an earthy-flavoured dried bean completely different from the better-known chinese black beans (fermented soybeans).
borlotti also called roman beans or pink beans, can be eaten fresh or dried. Interchangeable with pinto beans due to their similarity in appearance – pale pink or beige with dark red streaks.
broad also called fava, windsor and horse beans; available dried, fresh, canned and frozen. Fresh should be peeled twice (discarding both the outer long green pod and the beige-green tough inner shell); frozen beans have had their pods removed but the beige shell still needs to be removed.
butter cans labelled butter beans are, in fact, cannellini beans. Confusingly butter is also another name for lima beans, sold both dried and canned; a large beige bean with a mealy texture and mild taste.
cannellini small white bean similar in appearance and flavour to other varieties (great northern, navy or haricot). Available dried or canned.
kidney medium-size red bean, slightly floury in texture yet sweet in flavour; sold dried or canned.

lima large, flat kidney-shaped, beige dried and canned beans. Also known as butter beans.
white a generic term we use for canned or dried cannellini, haricot, navy or great northern beans.

BEEF
blade taken from the shoulder; isn't as tender as other cuts so needs slow cooking for best results.
cheek the cheek muscle. A very tough and lean cut of meat; often used for braising or slow cooking to produce a tender result.
chuck inexpensive cut from the neck and shoulder area; good minced and slow-cooked.
corned also called corned silverside; little fat, cut from the upper leg and cured. Sold cryovac-packed in brine.
gravy boneless stewing beef from shin; slow-cooked, imbues stocks, soups and casseroles with a gelatine richness. Cut crossways, with bone in, is osso buco.
minced also known as ground beef.
ox kidney originally from the ox but now likely to be from any beef cattle.
oxtail a flavourful cut originally sections of the tail of an ox but today more likely to be from any beef cattle; requires long, slow cooking so it is perfect for curries and stews.
rib roast a roast cut from the rib section that may contain two to seven rib bones. Also known as a prime, or standing rib roast.

BICARBONATE OF SODA also known as baking soda.

BOUQUET GARNI a bundle of herbs, usually tied together with string, used to flavour soups, stocks and casseroles. Ingredients vary but usually include bay leaf, parsley and thyme. Remove bouquet before serving.

BUK CHOY also known as bok choy, pak choi, chinese white cabbage or chinese chard; has a fresh, mild mustard taste. Use stems and leaves, stir-fried or braised. Baby buk choy, also known as pak kat farang or shanghai bok choy, is much smaller and more tender.

CAPERS the grey-green buds of a warm climate shrub, sold either dried and salted or pickled in a vinegar brine; tiny young ones, called baby capers, are available bottled in brine or dried in salt.

CAPSICUM Also called pepper or bell pepper. Discard seeds and membranes before use.

CARDAMOM a spice native to India and used extensively in its cuisine; can be purchased in pod, seed or ground.

CHICKEN
drumstick leg with skin and bone intact.
maryland leg and thigh still connected in a single piece; bones and skin intact.
thigh skin and bone intact
thigh cutlet thigh with skin and bone intact; sometimes found skinned with bone intact.
thigh fillet thigh with skin and bone removed.

CHILLIES use rubber gloves when handling fresh chillies as they can burn your skin. We use unseeded chillies because seeds contain the heat; use fewer chillies rather than seed the lot.
cayenne pepper a long, extremely hot, dried, ground red chilli native to South America.
chipotle pronounced cheh-pot-lay. Dried and smoked jalapeño chilli. Has a deep, intensely smoky flavour, the chipotle is a dark brown in colour and wrinkled in appearance.
flakes also sold as crushed chilli; dehydrated deep-red extremely fine slices and whole seeds.
jalapeño pronounced hah-lah-pen-yo. Fairly hot, medium-sized, plump, green chilli; available pickled, sold canned or bottled, and fresh.
long green any unripened chilli.
long red available both fresh and dried; a generic term used for a moderately hot, long, thin chilli.
powder can be used as a substitute for fresh chillies (½ teaspoon ground chilli powder to 1 medium chopped fresh chilli).
red thai also known as "scuds", "serrano" or "bird's eye" chillies; tiny, very hot and bright red.

CHINESE COOKING WINE also called shao hsing or chinese rice wine; made from fermented rice, wheat and sugar. Substitute mirin or sherry.

CHORIZO sausage of Spanish origin, made of coarsely ground pork and highly seasoned.

CHOY SUM a member of the buk choy family; easy to identify with its long stems and yellow flowers.

COCOA POWDER also known as unsweetened cocoa; cocoa beans (cacao seeds) that have been fermented, roasted, shelled, ground into powder then cleared of most of the fat content.

COCONUT

cream obtained from the first pressing of the coconut flesh alone, without the addition of water; the second pressing (less rich) is coconut milk. Available canned or dried.

milk not the liquid found inside the fruit, which is called coconut juice, but the liquid from the second pressing of the flesh of a mature coconut.

shredded strips of dried coconut flesh.

CORIANDER Also called cilantro, pak chee or chinese parsley; bright-green-leafed herb with both pungent aroma and taste. Coriander seeds are dried and sold either whole or ground.

CREAM we always use fresh cream unless otherwise stated.

pouring also known as pure cream. It has no additives and contains a minimum fat content of 35 per cent. If a recipe calls for an unspecified cream, this is the one we use.

sour a thick, commercially cultured sour cream with a minimum fat content of 35 per cent.

thickened also known as heavy cream, this is a whipping cream that contains a thickener. It has a minimum fat content of 35 per cent.

EGGS we use large chicken eggs weighing an average of 60g unless stated otherwise in the recipes in this book. if a recipe calls for raw or barely cooked eggs, exercise caution if there is a salmonella problem in your area, particularly in food eaten by children and pregnant women.

FISH SAUCE see sauces

FIVE-SPICE POWDER (chinese five-spice) although the ingredients vary it's usually a fragrant mixture of ground cinnamon, cloves, star anise, sichuan pepper and fennel seeds.

FLOUR

cornflour also known as cornstarch. Available made from corn or wheat; used for thickening.

plain also known as all-purpose; unbleached wheat flour is the best for baking: the gluten content ensures a strong dough, for a light result.

self-raising all-purpose plain or wholemeal flour with baking powder and salt added; make with plain white or wholemeal flour with baking powder in the proportion of 1 cup flour to 2 teaspoons baking powder.

GALANGAL also known as ka or lengkaus if fresh and laos if dried and powdered; a root, similar to ginger with a hot-sour citrusy flavour.

GARAM MASALA literally meaning blended spices in its northern Indian place of origin; cardamom, cinnamon, cloves, coriander, fennel and cumin, roasted and ground together.

GHEE clarified butter; with the milk solids removed, this fat has a high smoking point so can be heated to a high temperature without burning. Used in Indian recipes.

GINGER

fresh also called green or root ginger; the gnarled root of a tropical plant.

ground also called powdered ginger; used as a flavouring in baking but cannot be substituted for fresh ginger.

GOLDEN SYRUP a by-product of refined sugarcane; pure maple syrup or honey can be substituted. Treacle is more viscous, and has a stronger flavour and aroma than golden syrup.

HOISIN SAUCE see sauces

KAFFIR LIME LEAVES also known as bai magrood and looks like two glossy dark green leaves joined end to end. Sold fresh, dried or frozen; fresh lime peel may be substituted.

KECAP MANIS see sauces

KUMARA The Polynesian name of an orange-fleshed sweet potato often confused with yam; good baked, boiled, mashed or fried.

LAMB

easy-carve leg lamb leg with all but the shank bone removed for stress-free carving.

leg cut from the hindquarter; can be boned, butterflied, rolled and tied, or cut into dice.

minced ground lamb.

neck chops chops cut from the neck, ideal for stewing, braising and making stock.

shanks, french-trimmed also known as drumsticks or frenched shanks. The gristle and bone end are discarded and the meat trimmed.

shoulder large, tasty piece with much connective tissue so is best pot-roasted or braised. Can be cut into dice and makes good mince.

LEMON GRASS also known as takrai, serai or serah. A lemon-scented, aromatic tropical grass; the white lower part of the stem is used.

LENTILS (red, brown, yellow) dried pulses often identified by and named after their colour.

MAPLE SYRUP distilled from the sap of sugar maple trees found only in Canada and the USA. Maple-flavoured syrup is not a substitute.

MARSALA a fortified Italian wine recognisable by its intense amber colour and complex aroma.

MUSHROOMS

button small, cultivated white mushrooms with a mild flavour. If mushroom type is unspecified, always use button mushrooms.

swiss brown also known as roman or cremini. Brown mushrooms with full-bodied flavour.

OIL

olive made from ripened olives. Extra virgin and virgin are the first and second press, respectively, of the olives and are therefore considered the best; the apellation"light" refers to taste not fat levels.

peanut pressed from ground peanuts; the most commonly used oil in Asian cooking for its capacity to handle high heat without burning.

ONIONS

baby also known as pickling onions and cocktail onions; baby brown onions, larger than shallots.

brown and white are interchangeable, however white onions have a more pungent flesh.

green also known as scallion or (incorrectly) shallot; an immature onion picked before the bulb has formed, with a white base and a long, green edible stalk.

red also known as spanish, red spanish or bermuda onion; a sweet, large, purple-red onion.

shallots also called french shallots, golden shallots or eschalots; small brown-skinned elongated members of the onion family.

PANCETTA see pork

PAPRIKA ground dried red capsicum (bell pepper); available sweet, hot, mild and smoked.

PISTACHIOS delicately flavoured green nuts inside hard shells. We always use shelled nuts.

POLENTA also known as cornmeal; a cereal made from dried corn (maize).

POPPY SEEDS small, dried, bluish-grey seeds, with crunchy texture and nutty flavour.

PORK
american-style spareribs trimmed mid-loin ribs.
belly fatty cut sold in rashers or in a piece, with or without rind or bone.
ham hock the lower portion of the leg; includes the meat, fat and bone. Most have been cured and smoked.
neck sometimes called pork scotch, boneless cut from the foreloin.
pancetta an Italian unsmoked bacon, pork belly cured in salt and spices then rolled into a sausage shape and dried for several weeks.
pickled brine-cured cut, neck (from the foreloin) or shoulder is typical.
speck smoked pork.

POTATOES
baby new potatoes also known as chats; not a separate variety but an early harvest with very thin skin. Serve unpeeled steamed, or in salads.
kipfler small, finger-shaped, nutty flavour; great baked and in salads.

PRESERVED LEMON whole or quartered salted, preserved lemons. Use the rind only and rinse well under cold water before using.

QUINCE yellow-skinned fruit with hard texture and tart taste; long cooking makes the flesh deep pink.

RICE
arborio small, round grain rice well-suited to absorb a large amount of liquid; the high level of starch makes it especially suitable for risottos, giving the dish its classic creaminess.
basmati a white, fragrant long-grained rice; the grains fluff up beautifully when cooked. It should be washed several times before cooking.
jasmine or thai jasmine, is a long-grained white rice recognised by its perfumed quality; moist in texture, it clings together after cooking.
long-grain elongated grains that remain separate when cooked.

SAFFRON stigma of a member of the crocus family, available ground or in strands; imparts a yellow-orange colour to food once infused.

SAUCES
fish called naam pla on the label if Thai-made, nuoc naam if Vietnamese; the two are almost identical. Made from pulverised salted fermented fish; has a pungent smell and taste.
hoisin a thick, sweet and spicy chinese barbecue sauce made from fermented soybeans, onions and garlic; used as a marinade or baste.
kecap manis a dark, thick sweet soy sauce used in South-East Asian cuisines.
light soy sauce fairly thin in consistency and, while paler than the others, the saltiest tasting. Not to be confused with salt-reduced soy sauce.
soy sauce also known as sieu; made from fermented soybeans. We use a mild Japanese soy sauce unless indicated otherwise. It's possibly the best table soy.
tomato pasta sauce a prepared tomato-based sauce (sometimes called ragu or sugo on the label); comes in varying degrees of thickness and with different flavourings.
worcestershire sauce thin, dark-brown spicy sauce; used as a seasoning for meat, gravies and cocktails, and as a condiment.

SHRIMP PASTE also known as kapi, trasi, belacan and blachan; a strong-scented, very firm preserved paste made of salted dried shrimp. It should be chopped, then wrapped in foil and roasted before use.

SPECK see pork

SPINACH also known as english spinach and incorrectly, silver beet.

STAR ANISE dried star-shaped pod with an astringent aniseed flavour; used to flavour stocks and marinades. Available whole and ground.

SUGAR we use coarse, granulated table sugar, or crystal sugar, unless otherwise specified.
caster also known as superfine or finely granulated table sugar.
dark brown a moist, dark brown sugar with a rich, distinctive full flavour from molasses syrup.
light brown a very soft, finely granulated sugar that retains molasses for its colour and flavour.

palm also called nam tan pip, jaggery, jawa or gula melaka; made from the sap of the sugar palm tree. Use brown sugar if unavailable.

TAMARIND CONCENTRATE tamarind juice distilled into a condensed paste. Gives a sweet-sour taste to marinades, pastes and sauces.

TOMATOES
canned whole peeled tomatoes in natural juices; available crushed, chopped or diced. Unless otherwise specified, use the tomatoes undrained.
cherry also known as tiny tim or tom thumb tomatoes; small and round.
paste triple-concentrated tomato puree used to flavour soups, stews and sauces.
puree canned pureed tomatoes; substitute with fresh peeled and pureed tomatoes.

TOULOUSE SAUSAGE essential ingredient of a French cassoulet, a garlic and herb-laden coarse sausage.

TURMERIC also called kamin; is a rhizome related to galangal and ginger. Must be grated or pounded to release its aroma and flavour. Fresh can be substituted with dried powder.

VANILLA
bean dried, long, thin pod from a tropical golden orchid; the minuscule black seeds inside the bean are used to impart a luscious flavour in baking and desserts.
extract obtained from vanilla beans infused in water; a non-alcoholic version of essence.

VEAL, SHIN gelatinous shin meat of a beef calf; sold thickly sliced and with bone-in as osso buco.

VERJUICE from the French vert jus or verjus meaning, "green juice". It is the unfermented, slightly acidic juice of semi-ripe red and white wine grapes.

YOGURT we use plain full-cream yogurt in our recipes unless specifically noted otherwise. If a recipe calls for low-fat yogurt we use one with a fat content of less than 0.2 per cent.

ZUCCHINI also called courgette; small, pale- or dark-green or yellow vegetable of the squash family. Its edible flowers can be stuffed.